IMAGES
of America

OAKLAND

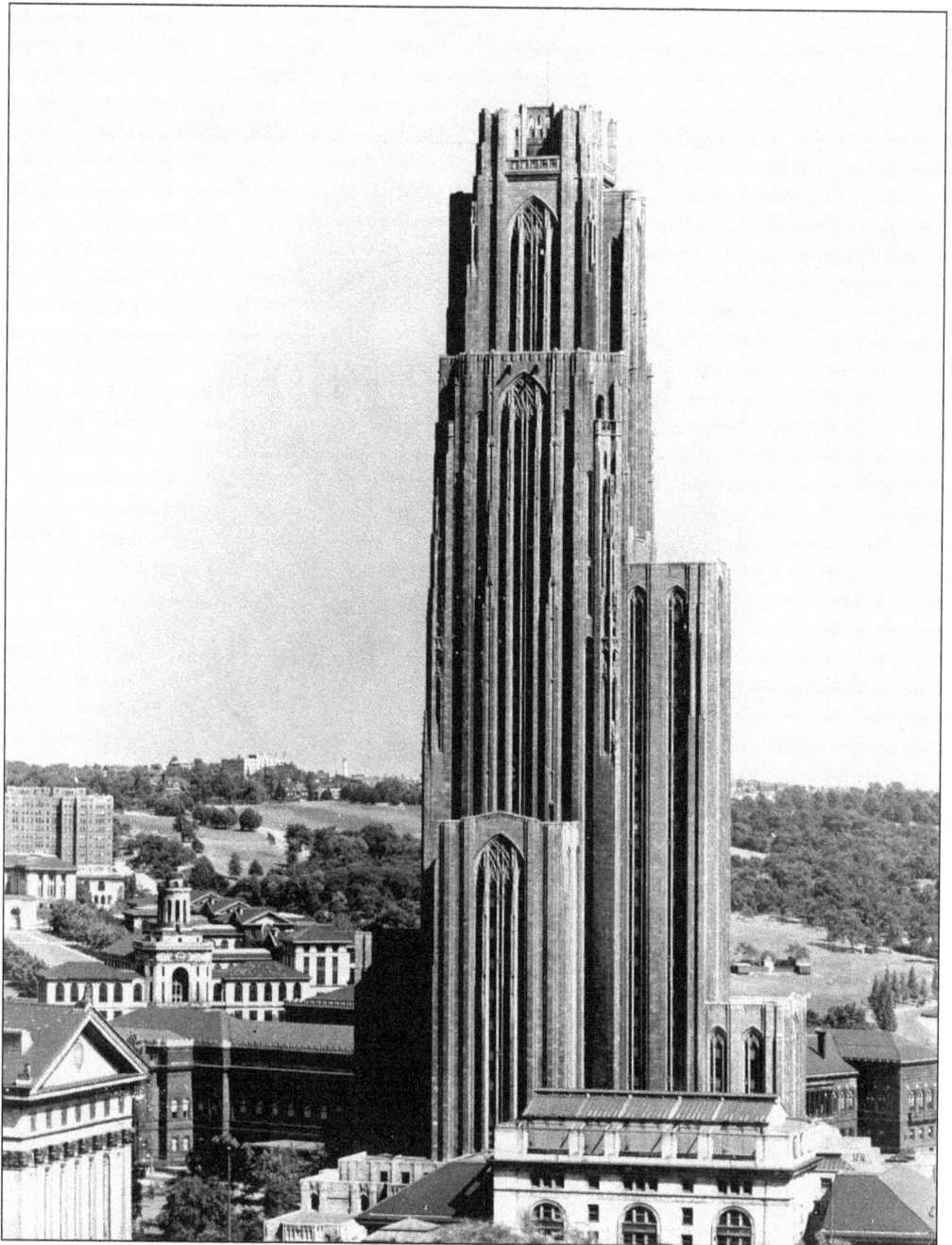

Oakland as Pittsburgh's showplace. (Pittsburgh City Photographer Collection, Archives Service Center, University of Pittsburgh.)

IMAGES
of *America*

OAKLAND

Walter C. Kidney
in partnership with the Pittsburgh History & Landmarks Foundation
and the Carnegie Library of Pittsburgh

ARCADIA
PUBLISHING

Published by Arcadia Publishing
Charleston, South Carolina

Library of Congress Catalog Card Number: 2005926081

For all general information contact Arcadia Publishing at:
Telephone 843-853-2070
Fax 843-853-0044
E-mail sales@arcadiapublishing.com
For customer service and orders:
Toll-Free 1-888-313-2665

Visit us on the Internet at www.arcadiapublishing.com

The old yields to the new. The time is around 1930, and the Henry Lloyd House is up on rails,
ready for removal from the place where the Mellon Institute of Industrial Research is to rise.
Across Bellefield Avenue, the University of Pittsburgh's Cathedral of Learning is receiving its
Gothic facing. (Archives Service Center, University of Pittsburgh, courtesy of the John Eichleay Jr.
Company of Pittsburgh.)

CONTENTS

Acknowledgments 6

1. An Overview of Oakland 7

2. Early Oakland 11

3. Schenley Park 27

4. Carnegie Library of Pittsburgh and Carnegie Institute 39

5. Carnegie Institute of Technology 51

6. Pittsburgh's Showplace 57

7. Schenley Farms 81

8. The University of Pittsburgh 87

9. The Medical Center 101

10. An Oakland Miscellany 109

ACKNOWLEDGMENTS

We thank Carol Robinson, a trustee of the Carnegie Library of Pittsburgh, for working in partnership with the author and the Pittsburgh History & Landmarks Foundation, and we thank the many members of the foundation whose contributions made this publication possible.

The following institutions and individuals were most helpful in securing the images for this book: Gil Pietrzak and Barry Chad of the Carnegie Library of Pittsburgh; Miriam Meislik of the Archives Service Center, University of Pittsburgh; staff members of the Library and Archives Division, Historical Society of Western Pennsylvania, Pittsburgh; Jennie Benford of the Carnegie Mellon University Archives; Martin Aurand of the Carnegie Mellon University Architecture Archives; Kathryn Miller Haines of the University of Pittsburgh's Center for American Music; Caitlain LeDonne of the Carnegie Museum of Art; Kenneth A. White of the Catholic Diocese of Pittsburgh; Mary A. McDonough, who lent us nine plates from 1914 issues of *The Builder*; Stanley Karas, who lent us two postcards from his collection; and George F. Eichleay of the John Eichleay Jr. Company of Pittsburgh, for giving us permission to use the photograph on page 4.

An aerial photograph taken about 1923 shows Oakland in the process of development. Two notable features, soon to come, are still missing: Pitt Stadium and the Cathedral of Learning. In the future, the former would stand out in any aerial view of the whole city, and the latter would be Oakland's most conspicuous feature. (Aerial Photographs of Pittsburgh, Archives Service Center, University of Pittsburgh.)

One

AN OVERVIEW OF OAKLAND

Oakland has always been a heterogeneous area, and its boundaries debatable. Among the roles it has played have been those of villa colony, entertainment center, municipal showplace, and simply another place to live in, in greater or lesser comfort. If you accept the boundaries assumed here, it has three universities, a medical center, and houses ranging, at various periods, from mansion to hovel. People have flocked to Oakland besides for baseball, football, basketball, ice-skating, opera, and the Pittsburgh Symphony.

As to its boundaries: to the west lies Soho, what is left of an industrial neighborhood, with the Golden Triangle, Pittsburgh's downtown, about two miles further west. The Hill neighborhood rises to overlook Oakland from the northwest. Oakland can be said to extend a half mile north from its main part along Bigelow Boulevard, which winds around the northern side of the Hill on its way to town. To the northeast is Shadyside, which can be assumed—or can it?—to start at Neville Street, while Squirrel Hill and Greenfield adjoin Oakland to the east. For this book's purposes, Carnegie Mellon University and Schenley Park are assumed to be wholly in Oakland, though there could be dispute on the matter. To the southwest lies the shore of the Monongahela River, where the Pittsburgh Works of Jones & Laughlin Steel long existed. This lies well below the plateau, hillside, and ravine territory of Oakland, but is part of it in a way, especially since steelworkers used to live on the edges of the bluff, and trudge down and up Pittsburgh's famous public steps twice daily.

This *c.* 1934 view gives a good idea of this varied neighborhood and its irregular perimeter. Near the center is the University of Pittsburgh's Cathedral of Learning, which is 535 feet high, and by far Oakland's tallest building. It is not yet complete in this picture, and its attendant structures, the Heinz Chapel and the Stephen Foster Memorial, are not yet begun. Just beyond the Cathedral of Learning is Fifth Avenue, running between the Golden Triangle, out of the picture to the left, and various East End neighborhoods beyond the picture to the lower right. Beyond, to the center right, is the Schenley Farms residential neighborhood. Just this side of the Cathedral of Learning is Forbes Street (later, Avenue), running between the Triangle and Squirrel Hill. Across Forbes from the Cathedral of Learning is the dark and sprawling Carnegie Institute and Carnegie Library of Pittsburgh, with Schenley Plaza to its left. At the bottom left is Schenley Park, and at the bottom center is the Carnegie Institute of Technology, which today is Carnegie Mellon University. These are separated from Schenley Plaza by Junction Hollow, which is crossed here by the Schenley Bridge. (Carnegie Library of Pittsburgh.)

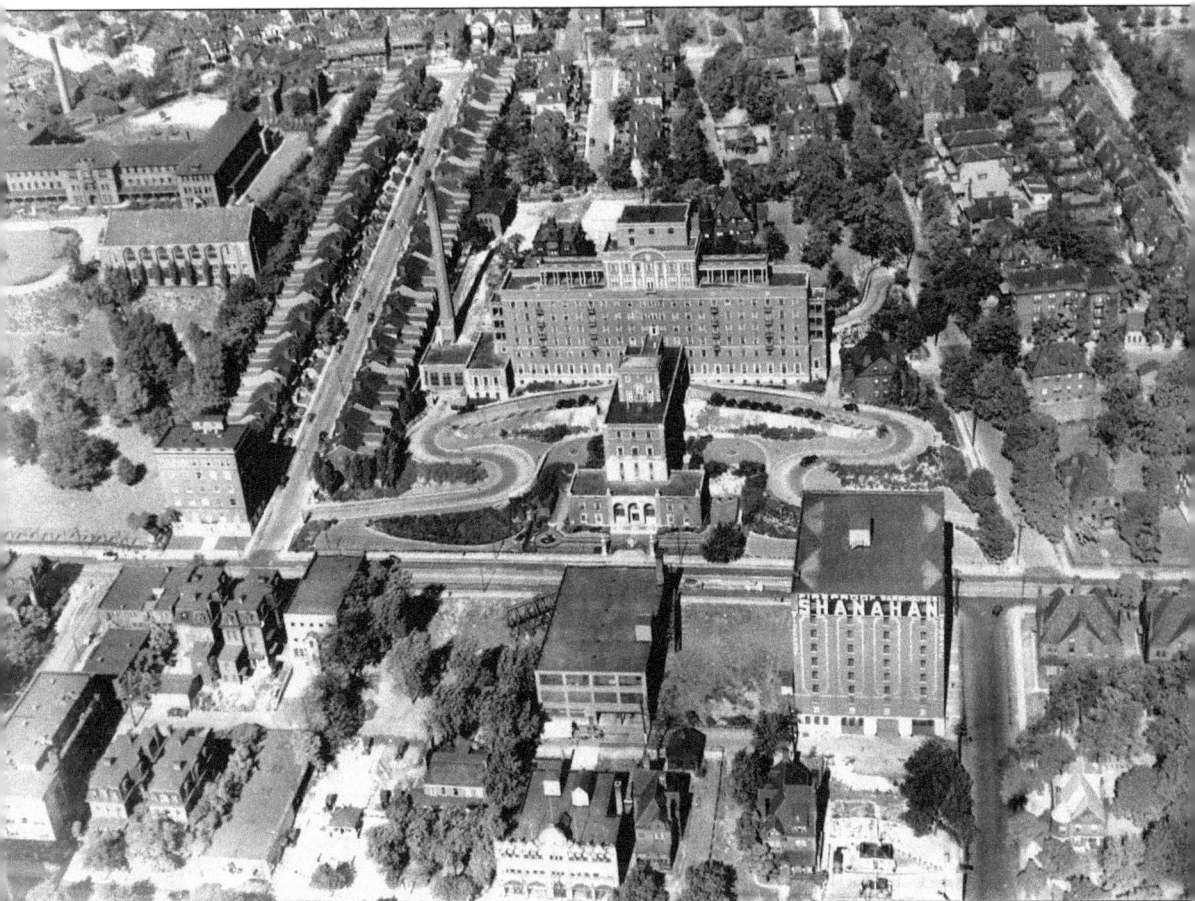

This view from the late 1920s of the Montefiore Hospital area gives some idea of Oakland's mixed character. Fifth Avenue runs across the picture. In the upper left is Mount Mercy, a women's school that today is Carlow University. To the right of the school is Chesterfield Road, a picturesquely fronted double-house row. Montefiore Hospital, brand-new, appears grandly above the street, taking the place of the old Eichbaum House that had survived until recently. Behind the hospital, almost hidden, is the Reilly House, a Second Empire mansion of the 1870s, and above that is Buffalo Street, a little street of closely spaced houses from the 1900s. To the right of the hospital are Darragh and Lothrop Streets, middle-class residential, and at the upper right corner just a little of the old H. K. Porter estate, in the process of becoming an area of medical buildings. South of Fifth Avenue are Victorian houses, industrial buildings, and a Gothic-styled Croatian fraternal association. Among its trees, too, is the Coltart House, a villa remaining from the 1840s. (The Historical Society of Western Pennsylvania.)

This 1953 view at the eastern edge of Oakland shows the neighborhood in transition. St. Paul's Cathedral has strange neighbors, just like Montefiore Hospital. Directly across Fifth Avenue, at the bottom of the picture, is a house in the old East Pittsburgh development that a map of the 1870s assigns to a "Mr. K." Directly across Craig Street, sharing a large lot with a pair of billboards, is the A. A. Carrier villa of the 1870s that lasted until 1956. We will return to this, as we will to the large industrial structure beside it—a streetcar barn that in 1953 housed a sports arena, the Gardens. Across Fifth Avenue from this strangely underused property was the Fairfax, a c. 1925 apartment house with a thin application of Elizabethan detailing. Beyond all these, Ellsworth Avenue angles off into another neighborhood; the Episcopal Church of the Ascension, at Ellsworth's meeting with Neville Street, marks the start of Shadyside. (Carnegie Museum of Art, Pittsburgh; gift of the Carnegie Library of Pittsburgh.)

Two

EARLY OAKLAND

First, the name will be discussed. An early settler, William Eichbaum (whose surname translates to "oaktree" in German), evidently did *not* give this early suburb its name; the moniker had already been applied to the area by 1839, a year before Eichbaum settled there.

As to how and why Oakland was developed: descendants of William Penn had a large "manor" in Western Pennsylvania, which included a large part of the present-day Oakland. Some of this was sold in 1787 to Robert Neill (whose log house is still in Oakland's Schenley Park), and some to Edward Smith in 1791. The two sold land to Gen. John O'Hara, who left it to his daughter Mary. She married William Croghan and they had a daughter, also named Mary, who was born in 1826. This second Mary, 16 years old and attending a girls' school on Staten Island, met and married Capt. Edward Schenley, 40 years old and twice widowed. The couple settled in England, though they returned occasionally. After 1880 the Schenleys had complete control of the Croghan and O'Hara holdings. Mary preferred to lease rather than sell or improve the land, and it remained remarkably undeveloped in the midst of increasing urban density as the end of the century approached.

To the west of the Schenley land, Edward Smith sold land to Charles Taylor, who in 1836 subdivided his land as "country estates." Several members of the new Third Presbyterian Church downtown bought lands for villas: enough of them that this section, some two miles from the smoke and clamor of town, was once called the Third Church Colony.

South of the Third Church Colony, Edward Craft (or Crafts) developed a large area that became known as Linden Grove. This was a disorganized, gradual assemblage of large, closely spaced houses and row houses that developed bit by bit throughout the first quarter of the 20th century.

East of the Schenley land was a farm called Bellefield, the property of the early newspaper publisher and historian Neville B. Craig. Edward Dithridge bought much of the Craig estate in 1851 and laid out an area of small lots that he called East Pittsburgh. His layout survives on both sides of South Craig Street.

At first Oakland was part of Pitt Township, but was annexed to Pittsburgh in 1868. Communications between Oakland and downtown Pittsburgh, two miles to the west, and East Liberty, two miles to the east and north, affected development as those areas prospered. In 1859 a horsecar line started to run between downtown and East Liberty by way of Fifth Avenue. This was replaced in 1888 by cable cars, which ran until 1896, when the Fifth Avenue line went electric.

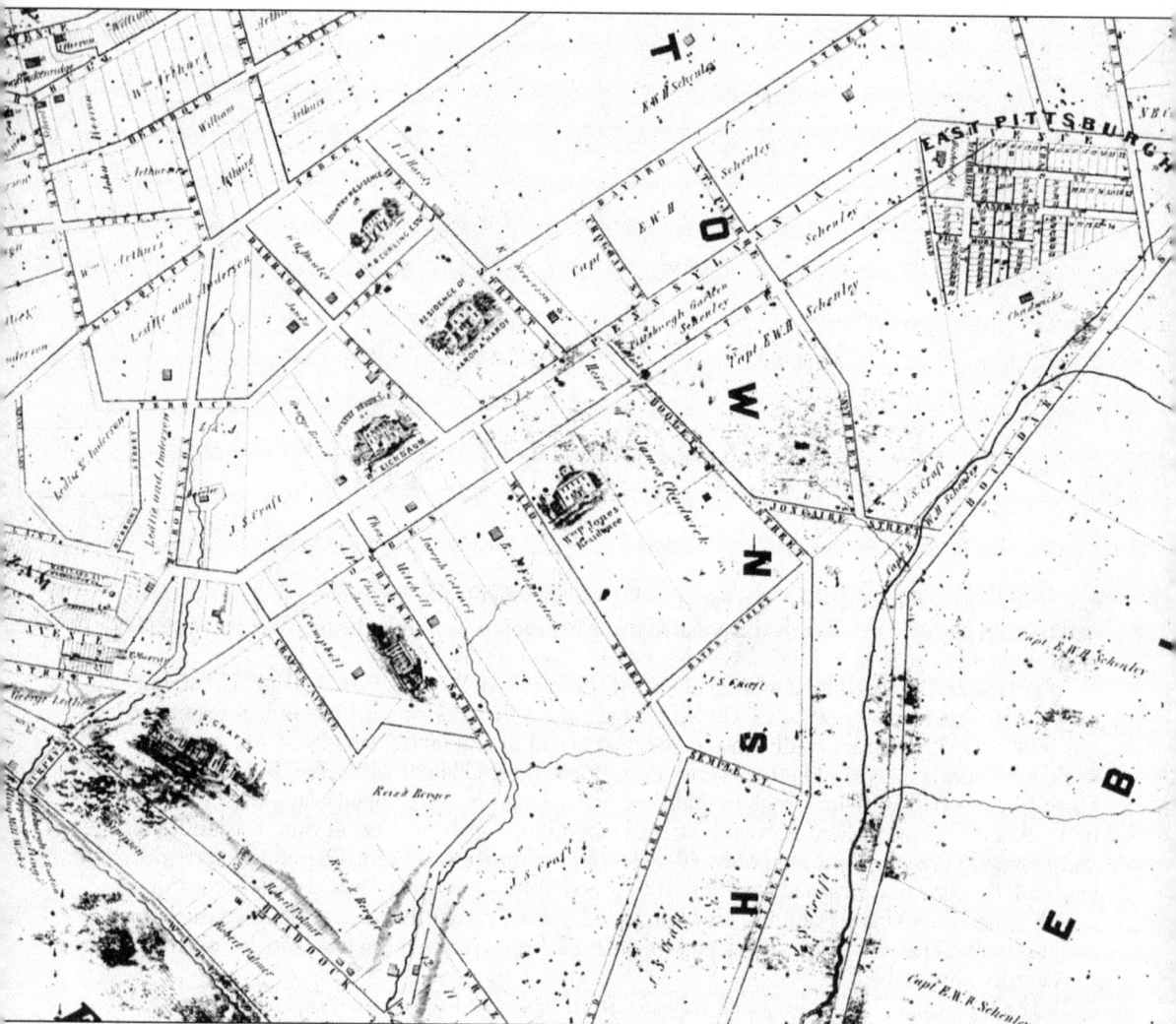

The R. E. McGowin map of 1852 shows Oakland's early state. Pennsylvania Avenue (today, Fifth Avenue) runs northeasterly with Forbes Street below it. Villas appear in the Third Church Colony area and south of Forbes, but the Schenley lands beyond Bouquet Street are unimproved. Further along, at the eastern edge, come Bellefield and the small lots of East Pittsburgh. (Pittsburgh History & Landmarks Foundation.)

This is a portrait of Mary Schenley (1826–1903) in old age. She seems to have retained a soft spot for her birthplace in later years; she gave 300 acres for Schenley Park in 1889, as well as land for the Western Pennsylvania Institution for the Blind. In 1894 she gave the downtown Blockhouse, the sole remainder of the 18th-century Fort Pitt, to the Daughters of the American Revolution. (Carnegie Library of Pittsburgh.)

This log house was still standing in the four-year-old Schenley Park in 1893, the property of one of Robert Neill's neighbors. With its squared logs and relatively well-wrought joints it is a real house, not a crudely assembled cabin, but even in 1893 it showed signs of deterioration, and today no longer exists. Neill's own log house remains, however, restored. (Pittsburgh History & Landmarks Foundation.)

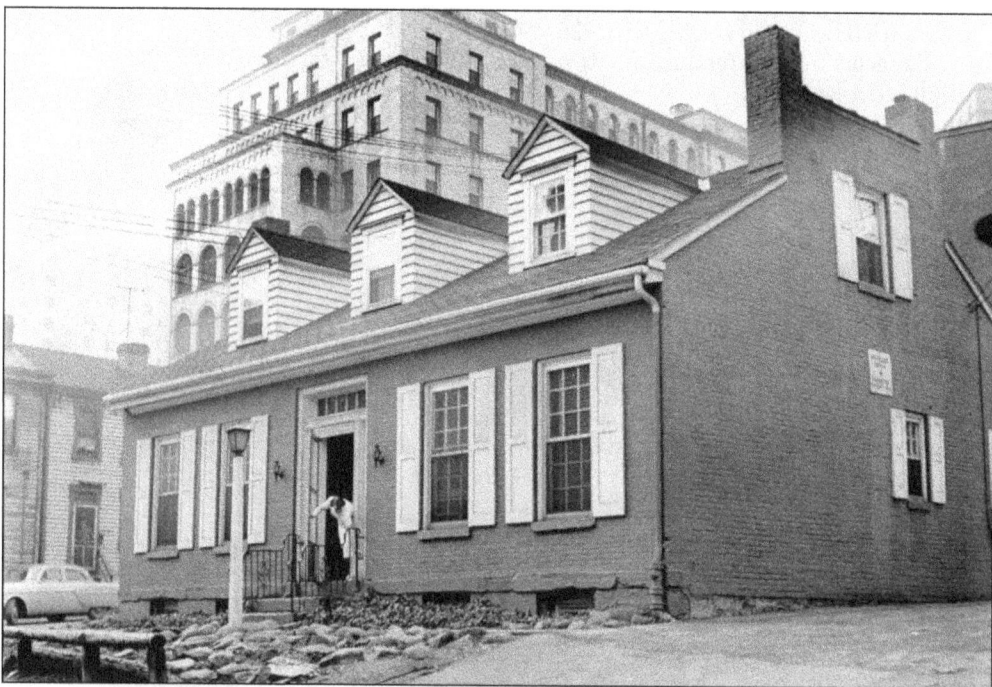

Judging from the 1852 map, this was the property of someone named Greerson: a house that existed, surprisingly, into the 1950s when this picture was taken. Its doorway, with an over-door light and sidelights, and its paired chimneys sunken into the wall suggest a very early date, quite possibly the 1840s. Behind it, across DeSoto Street, is Children's Hospital. (Carnegie Library of Pittsburgh.)

The Joseph Coltart House was built in 1843, across the road from William Eichbaum's own villa. This photograph shows the rear of the house. The front, toward Fifth Avenue, had a pretentious wooden porch in the Grecian Doric order. In its last days, the Coltart House belonged to the local YMCA. The structure came down in the 1960s. (Pittsburgh History & Landmarks Foundation.)

This 1876 lithograph from a history of Allegheny County shows the villa that William Eichbaum built in the 1840s. Here we see the residence after it had passed into the hands of John Moorhead, an ironmaster. It was probably Moorhead who added the cast-iron verandahs on the side wings. The house lasted into the 20th century, and was replaced in the late 1920s by Montefiore Hospital. The mansarded house at the top of the rise, owned by John C. Reilly, was built not long before this lithograph was made and stood immediately behind Montefiore until around 1950. In the foreground, on Fifth Avenue, a horsecar of the Pittsburgh, Oakland & East Liberty Railway passes, headed for town. (Pittsburgh History & Landmarks Foundation.)

The Maples, at Forbes and Halket Streets, was built by Asa P. Childs, an incorporator of the Third Presbyterian Church, and later passed into the hands of the prominent politician Christopher Lyman Magee. Its grounds were occupied after 1915 by the Elizabeth Steel Magee Hospital. (Carnegie Library of Pittsburgh.)

Next door stood Alicia, the house of Charles J. Clarke. It was noted for its beautiful grounds and its grand social occasions. Early in the 20th century, it was first converted into an armory and later was razed to make way for a Pittsburgh Railways trolley barn. (Carnegie Library of Pittsburgh.)

16

A neighbor of The Maples and Alicia, in their last days, was St. Peter's Episcopal Church, at Forbes Street and Craft Avenue. Whether the church can be considered part of early Oakland is a matter of opinion. It was constructed downtown at Fifth and Grant in 1852, to the designs of the Philadelphia architect John Notman, as a "chapel of ease" for Trinity Episcopal Church. The building was designed scrupulously to satisfy the requirements of the Ecclesiological Society in England for correct Anglican architecture. In 1901, Henry Clay Frick paid to have it disassembled and rebuilt in Oakland to make way for his new headquarters building. In the reconstruction, a porch was added in front. Few people were attending the church by the 1980s, and it came down in 1990. (Pittsburgh History & Landmarks Foundation.)

Frick Acres, the 14-acre area where the Cathedral of Learning was to rise, was long Schenley land but was already being occupied by 1872, as a map of that year indicates. The mid-Victorian Browne House appears to date from about 1860: an unfancy but ample Italianate house, one of several houses on the block. (University Archives, University of Pittsburgh.)

This carriage party of around 1905 is unexplained, though it seems likely that they are members of the Browne family. The land, along with all the land adjoining, had been amassed by Henry Clay Frick for eventual development. The Browne House would stay into the 1920s, making way at last for the Cathedral of Learning. (University Archives, University of Pittsburgh.)

Here is an interior of the Browne House, with no date given. Some of the fixtures seem to be electric and the furniture is Georgian in appearance, so early 20th century seems likely. (University Archives, University of Pittsburgh.)

The Davison House at Fifth Avenue and Craig Street was a plain, typical piece of mid-Victorian vernacular, a little more vertical in its proportions and lower-pitched in its roof than a late-18th-century house might have been, but not looking essentially different. The porch, though, is a rather fancy addition from late in the century. (The Historical Society of Western Pennsylvania.)

The William Tate House remains in the old East Pittsburgh area, at Craig and Forbes, though hardly recognizable today. A boxy commercial annex now conceals almost everything on Forbes, though the mansard roof is still discernible. (The Historical Society of Western Pennsylvania.)

Isaac Hobbs & Sons was a Philadelphia architectural office that had much success in the Pittsburgh area, with 11 or possibly 12 buildings executed. The best known of these is the baroque-looking Dollar Savings Bank still in downtown Pittsburgh; the earliest Bellefield Presbyterian Church, erected in 1866, was another building of interest. Constructed of wood, although sanded in imitation of stone, the building burned in 1869. (Carnegie Library of Pittsburgh.)

The house that Isaac Hobbs built at Fifth and Craig for A. A. Carrier lasted until 1956, in its later days with the Duquesne Gardens sports arena and St. Paul's Cathedral as its neighbors. In his 1873 book *Architecture*, Hobbs notes, "We have seven dwellings and one church [the Bellefield Presbyterian] within view of this building." The house soon passed into the hands of Robert C. Schmertz, a glassmaker. (Carnegie Library of Pittsburgh.)

Next door, on Fifth, was a similar house by Hobbs built for S. S. Carrier, but this also soon changed hands. By 1876 it belonged to Jacob Reese. The two Carrier houses follow the popular mid-Victorian compositional formula also used in Alicia, with a basic L-shaped Italianate front, a mansarded tower in the re-entering angle, and several porches and bay windows. (Pittsburgh History & Landmarks Foundation.)

This house on the Grove Hill estate had a long history in one form or another. Built by Aaron A. Hardy and visible on the 1852 map, it passed into the hands of J. C. Bidwell and eventually into those of H. K. Porter, a locomotive manufacturer, who renamed the estate Oak Manor. In his possession it acquired an art gallery as a major annex, shown here. Eventually it became a faculty club for the University of Pittsburgh, and was razed in the early 1920s to afford land for the Medical Center. The property ran between Fifth Avenue and Terrace Street, and between what are now Lothrop and DeSoto Streets. On the property, by 1940, these were built: the Falk Clinic, Children's Hospital, and the triple building housing the Eye and Ear, Presbyterian, and Women's Hospital. Later on, a large nurses' residence and other structures were added. (Carnegie Library of Pittsburgh.)

Soho Curve was the nearest thing Oakland had to a distinct entrance, with Fifth Avenue winding as it does some 50 feet uphill from the Soho neighborhood to the west. The scene here is from around 1890, with Pittsburgh Traction cable cars making their way up and down at 12 miles an hour. The curve was the most difficult engineering challenge on the line, requiring 290 sheaves, whose covers are visible here, to keep the cables in place. The fantastic structure at the top of the rise, which was then called Mont Sainte Ursule, is the convent of the Ursuline Young Ladies Academy. (Carnegie Library of Pittsburgh.)

In 1889, Isaac Hobbs's Bellefield Presbyterian Church was replaced by this masonry work, designed by the young Pittsburgh architect Frederick John Osterling. Osterling was to become one of the city's most successful architects, at least in a business sense. The tower still stands at Fifth Avenue's bend at Bellefield Avenue, serving as an accent feature for a large modern office structure. (Pittsburgh History & Landmarks Foundation.)

This 1893 photograph shows the municipal bridge recently built to carry Halket Street over Cunliffe Hollow in Linden Grove. The design is a progressive one, a mixture of arch and cantilever. This hollow is no longer visible, and the area was absorbed into the Boulevard of the Allies extension, from downtown Pittsburgh to Schenley Park and Squirrel Hill, that was built in the 1920s. (Pittsburgh History & Landmarks Foundation.)

Here, in 1893, is Junction Hollow, a notable feature in the local geography. We are looking northward toward Forbes Street from the new Schenley Bridge, an instrument of the changes about to come. Among the most conspicuous of these changes will be Schenley Park, under development just out of view to the right, and the Carnegie Library, under construction just out of the picture to the left. The trolley car has just left the land that will soon be that of the Carnegie Institute of Technology; it is traveling to Oakland from Squirrel Hill. An innovation in 1893, the electric streetcar had by this time become the subject of an investment mania, with hundreds of local companies existing, at least on paper. (Pittsburgh History & Landmarks Foundation.)

Casey's Row, a Fifth Avenue development of frame and brick houses, was obviously intended as a respectable and rather glamorous addition to a developing area that very shortly would include the Carnegie Library, the First United Presbyterian Church, and the Hotel Schenley. Schenley Park, in addition, was not far away. Alas, the solid-looking houses were to last only about 15 years. The Pittsburgh Athletic Association and the Masonic Temple would replace them. (Pittsburgh History & Landmarks Foundation.)

Edward Manning Bigelow (1850–1916) was Pittsburgh's wily, embattled, sometimes idealistic director of public works who gave the city its first real parks, started a boulevard system, and eventually, created a safe water supply. He had the rare pleasure of living to see a statue of himself dedicated, in 1895, in Schenley Park. (The Historical Society of Western Pennsylvania.)

Three

SCHENLEY PARK

Oakland assumed the role of Pittsburgh's showplace between 1889 and a half century later, when its City Beautiful development came to a halt. Much of this development in the eastern part of the neighborhood was on Schenley land, which was at last sold. Mary Schenley had donated the land for Schenley Park in 1889—300 acres of it, or about two-thirds of the eventual total—and some of her remaining Oakland land had been sold or donated even before her death in 1903. But much Schenley land remained, most of it quite unimproved, until a Cleveland businessman, Franklin Nicola, wrought a series of remarkable changes.

Schenley Park was changed first. In 1889 two cities faced each other across the Allegheny River: Pittsburgh to the south, and Allegheny, a whole different municipality at that time, to the north. Allegheny, more progressive in some ways, had turned its 18th-century grazing commons into a greenbelt around the center of town; the new Allegheny Commons was a formal Victorian park, with fountains and flower beds. Pittsburgh, meanwhile, had one token park, on Second Avenue where there had been a market house. But by 1889, Pittsburgh's progressive director of public works, Edward Manning Bigelow, had resolved to bring parks to the city, partly to protect the water reservoirs and partly to bring the raw city some needed amenities.

There is a romantic story about the acquisition of the Mount Airy tract, with its plateaux and ravines, which Bigelow contemplated for a park. Having heard that a developer's agent was headed for London to make Mary Schenley an offer for the land, Bigelow rousted a friend from bed and somehow got him to board the same boat and race the agent—from Liverpool, presumably, then through the streets of London—to Mary Schenley's breakfast table. There, Bigelow's friend made his pitch, received her promise of the land, and then greeted the agent politely as he was leaving the Schenley house and the agent was coming in. The facts were apparently less romantic, with Bigelow accompanying his friend, who already had business relations with the Schenleys, and getting to London quite comfortably ahead of the agent.

Schenley Park was the first element of Pittsburgh's 50-year City Beautiful venture: not a formal terminal feature to a broad, axial boulevard as one might expect, but rather a romantic landscape, the civilizing of a wooded area with 300-foot differences of level. The first Schenley Bridge, the homely trestle shown here in 1893, connected the area near the Carnegie Library, under construction off to the left, with Schenley Park, under development to the right. (Pittsburgh History & Landmarks Foundation.)

William Falconer, an Englishman, was in charge of Schenley Park's landscaping. By 1893, the interior of the original 300 acres included the "Great Bend," where Serpentine Drive meets East Circuit Road. On the rise in the background is the Neill log house, built by Robert Neill around 1790. The house was starting to be venerated as an "old-timer" in the local historic scene. (Pittsburgh History & Landmarks Foundation.)

28

The Phipps Conservatory was a gift of Andrew Carnegie's boyhood friend and contemporary business partner, Henry Phipps, in 1893. The work of Lord & Burnham, greenhouse builders of Irvington, New York, it had an entrance block in a hybrid Romanesque style with classical details that led to a palm house, then to a system of wings that were added to later. In this view from 1899, the Carnegie Library, as it was originally designed, appears on the other side of Junction Hollow. (Pittsburgh History & Landmarks Foundation.)

A view from 1914 shows Phipps Conservatory's neighbors: its own carefully planted lawn; Schenley Drive; the rising lawn of Flagstaff Hill, a public gathering place of many uses; and finally, in the background, the buildings of Carnegie Tech (the Carnegie Institute of Technology), still under construction. (Pittsburgh City Photographer Collection, Archives Service Center, University of Pittsburgh.)

In this view inside the Phipps Conservatory, Mrs. Angie Means poses on a *Victoria regia* lily pad in one of the end pavilions. The photograph was taken around 1895—for a Masonic national convention, we understand. (Carnegie Library of Pittsburgh.)

Flower shows at Phipps Conservatory could be quite elaborate, as seen here in 1931, with a large model of a bungalow to establish the mood in one room. (Pittsburgh City Photographer Collection, Archives Service Center, University of Pittsburgh.)

The Phipps Hall of Botany, another gift of Henry Phipps, stands near the conservatory: a work in the Elizabethan style by Rutan & Russell. This is a view from 1910. The handsome old building remains, restored in 1999. (Pittsburgh City Photographer Collection, Archives Service Center, University of Pittsburgh.)

In the first few decades of Schenley Park's existence, there was a band shell in the area overlooking Junction Hollow; it is shown here around 1900. A walk past Phipps Conservatory and across the Panther Hollow Bridge brought the park-goer to this gentle lawn. The concerts seem to have been popular; here, not even a shower has kept people away. (Carnegie Library of Pittsburgh.)

Near the band shell was a swimming pool, here shown in 1921 on the occasion of its formal opening. (Pittsburgh City Photographer Collection, Archives Service Center, University of Pittsburgh.)

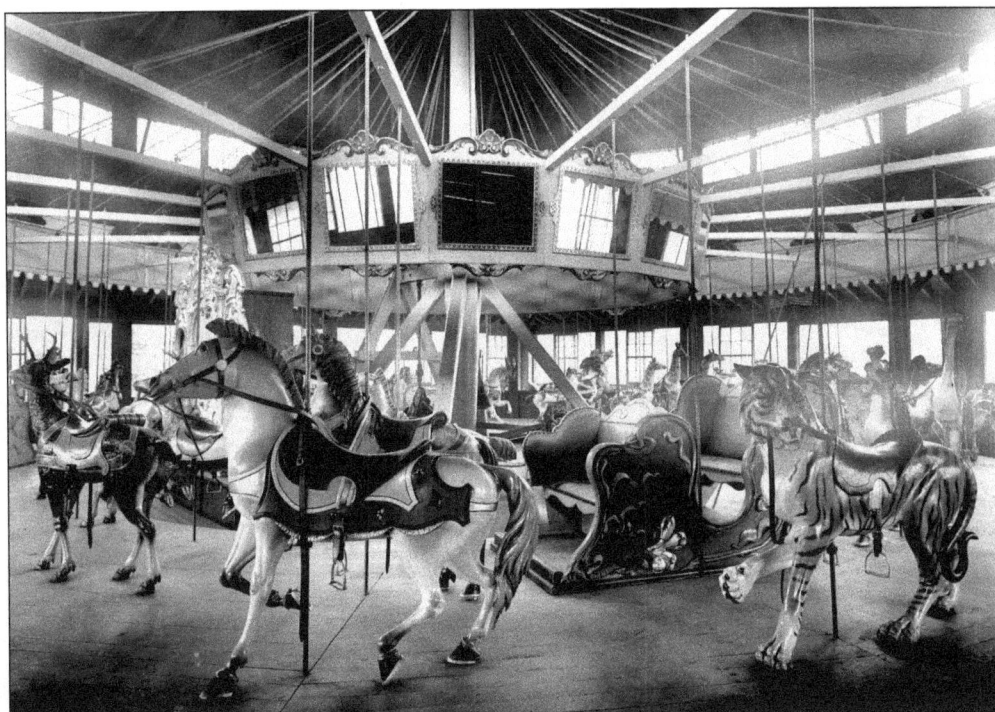

Elsewhere, in the heart of Schenley Park at the junction of several roads, was a merry-go-round. This view is from the summer of 1913. (Pittsburgh City Photographer Collection, Archives Service Center, University of Pittsburgh.)

Schenley Oval lay at one of the Park's highest places, about 350 feet above river level and with excellent views toward town. This picture from 1932 shows a harness race. A note says that the horse in the lead is Allan Jr., driven by Ed Wood. Admission seems to have been gratis, through the kindness of the Schenley Matinee Club. (Carnegie Library of Pittsburgh.)

Panther Hollow is a branch of Junction Hollow, extending eastward. In 1897, the second Schenley Bridge and the Panther Hollow Bridge were built with steel parabolic-arch main spans of identical design and dimensions—360-foot spans, 45-foot rise. These arches have been critically acclaimed as classics of their type for their economic, functional beauty. The rugged masonry abutments (which bear the marks of the masons who dressed their stones) differ somewhat in the two bridges. The engineer was a local man, H. B. Rust. In the foreground, in this scene from the early 20th century, is Panther Hollow Lake, used for rowing, fishing, and skating, with its boathouse. (Carnegie Library of Pittsburgh.)

The Panther Hollow Bridge, unlike the Schenley Bridge, bears sculptures on its abutments: four bronzes of "panthers" (actually, mountain lions) by Giuseppe Moretti, a monumental sculptor much in favor in Pittsburgh into the 1920s. (Carnegie Library of Pittsburgh.)

From 1969 comes this view of skating on Panther Hollow Lake, taken from Panther Hollow Bridge, 125 feet above, and looking toward Junction Hollow and its railroad line. (Pittsburgh City Photographer Collection, Archives Service Center, University of Pittsburgh.)

Another sculptural presence to be encountered in Schenley Park is a type of drinking fountain designed around 1935 by Frank Vittor, who replaced Giuseppe Moretti in the 1930s as Pittsburgh's monumental sculptor of choice. (Pittsburgh History & Landmarks Foundation.)

One feature of the developing park was a bridle path, and to carry this, two bridges were built in 1908. They were built of reinforced concrete but were faced with tufa, a white, porous rock found in some streams, that gave an appropriately rustic effect. (Carnegie Library of Pittsburgh.)

A memorial to the Pittsburgh industrialist George Westinghouse was commissioned by many of his loyal ex-employees and was dedicated in Schenley Park in 1930. It stands near one of the park's winding drives at the end of a lily pond. The architect was Henry Hornbostel, and the sculptors were Daniel Chester French and Paul Fjelde. The bearded Hornbostel is shown at the memorial with A. C. Humphrey, chairman of the Westinghouse Memorial Association, during the dedication ceremony. (Carnegie Mellon University Architecture Archives.)

This air show was given in Schenley Park in 1908, probably in connection with the city's sesquicentennial. (Pittsburgh History & Landmarks Foundation.)

A grand back entrance to Schenley Park was afforded in 1923 by the opening of the Beechwood Boulevard (or Greenfield) Bridge. The city architect, Stanley Roush, gave the bridge a grand treatment with steles, urns, and obelisks, which have not survived. This is the bridge when it was new. (Pittsburgh City Photographer Collection, Archives Service Center, University of Pittsburgh.)

Four

CARNEGIE LIBRARY
OF PITTSBURGH AND
CARNEGIE INSTITUTE

Andrew Carnegie (1835–1919) was arguably the richest man in the United States, if not in the world, after the sale of his interests to United States Steel in 1901. He has remained a controversial figure: a hard-driving employer, but a most generous philanthropist who helped fund libraries and cultural institutions that were free to the people.

In 1881, Carnegie had offered the City of Pittsburgh the first of the many public libraries he would build, but municipal officials declined, feeling that the city had not the money to maintain a library. Once Schenley Park was committed, Carnegie repeated his offer in 1890, with a site adjacent to the park in mind. This time the answer was yes, and Carnegie actually presented the City of Pittsburgh with an omnibus cultural building—a library, art museum, museum of natural history, meeting place for learned societies, and music hall, all under one roof—that was built between 1892 and 1895. But this first building quickly proved too small, and Carnegie paid to have it quadrupled in size between 1903 and 1907.

In 1898, two of the separate entities that had shared the building with the Carnegie Library—the Museum of Fine Arts and the Museum of Natural History—had merged to become Carnegie Institute. In the new building, the Carnegie Institute fronted on Forbes Street, and the Carnegie Library of Pittsburgh occupied the portion of the first building that remained visible from what today is Schenley Plaza.

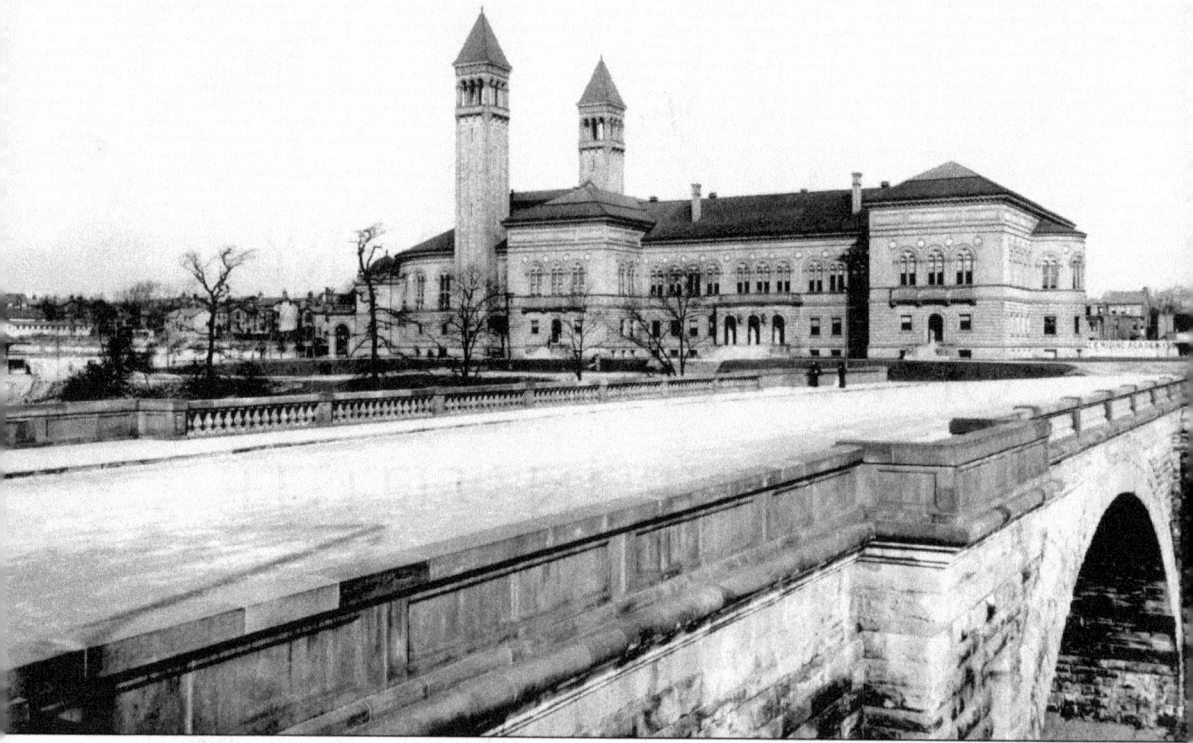

Basically the first design, by the Boston-Pittsburgh firm of Longfellow, Alden & Harlow, was a boxy 15th-century Italian palazzo, but Venetian campanili separated the reposeful, symmetrical library and museums from the rotund Music Hall that had its own entrance on Forbes Street. In the foreground in this view from 1899 is St. Pierre Ravine, a little branch of Junction Hollow that is spanned by the Bellefield Bridge, a new work in masonry by H. B. Rust. (Pittsburgh History & Landmarks Foundation.)

Here are two images from a c. 1900 postcard. The second conductor of the Pittsburgh Symphony, between 1898 and 1904, was none other than Victor Herbert, composer of *Babes in Toyland*, *The Red Mill*, and *Naughty Marietta*. The concert hall he used presented this face to Forbes Street before 1903. A portion of this old round front can still be seen in the basement of the present-day entrance block. (Pittsburgh History & Landmarks Foundation.)

This is the interior of the Music Hall in 1936, not much changed from its original state. (Carnegie Library of Pittsburgh.)

41

Dear Annie — Did you ever see this before? from Jessie

Hope you are enjoying yourself.

Carnegie Institute and Library, Pittsburg, Pa.

7-25-'06

This view from 1906 shows the enlarged Carnegie Institute-Carnegie Library of Pittsburgh building still under construction, with its sculptures not yet in place. In the 1903–1907 expansion, the part of the first building that faced St. Pierre Ravine was changed only in part, but everything on Forbes Street was new. The old Music Hall was encased in a monumental pavilion, and a balancing pavilion was created as the entrance to a new art museum space. The Museum of Natural History and new Halls of Sculpture and Architecture lay in between. The Carnegie Library came to occupy the whole original building apart from the Music Hall. The architects were Alden & Harlow, Pittsburgh successors to the original designers. (Pittsburgh History & Landmarks Foundation.)

This is the Forbes Street entrance facing up Bellefield Avenue, showing one of John Massey Rhind's sculptural groups over the Art Museum entrance and the elaborate copper cheneau (lost in the 1950s) that trimmed the roof parapets. This new front along Forbes Street struck a grander note than the original building along Schenley Plaza had. (Carnegie Library of Pittsburgh.)

This is the inside of the Bellefield Avenue entrance. The vestibule of the former main entrance was given similar detailing. The basic design is simple and lucid, but the richly figured bronze doors and the fish-scale patterns on the over-door lights and lamp globes hint at the lavishness to be found in the major spaces beyond. (Carnegie Library of Pittsburgh.)

Carnegie Library and McGee Memorial Fountain,
Pittsburg, Pa.

Here is the main front of the first building after the enlargement. The towers have been removed, and the wall system has been extended leftward. The former main entrance is now the entrance to the city's main Carnegie Library of Pittsburgh, and has been topped with a colonnade. (Pittsburgh History & Landmarks Foundation; courtesy of Stanley Karas.)

This monument, in memory of the politician Christopher Lyman Magee, was erected directly facing the Carnegie Library of Pittsburgh entrance. Dedicated in 1907, it had *Amor,* a bronze bas-relief by Augustus Saint-Gaudens, set in a stele designed by Henry Bacon, who was to design the Lincoln Memorial in Washington, D.C. (Pittsburgh History & Landmarks Foundation.)

Corridor towards Children's Department 2549

Inside the Library the stairs were realigned. The corridors maintain the serene Quattrocento simplicity of the original architecture, but the new stairs terminate in ceiling paintings of blue skies, surrounded with heavy baroque moldings. Here is a view down the Carnegie Library of Pittsburgh's first-floor main corridor after 1907. (Carnegie Library of Pittsburgh.)

45

The new foyer of the Music Hall was a place of the utmost pomp, with verde-antique columns and a richly figured ceiling, lavishly gilded. At one end Andrew Carnegie sits enthroned, accompanied by a motto: All is well since all grows better. (Pittsburgh History & Landmarks Foundation.)

The balancing feature for the Art Museum was this stair hall, with the *Apotheosis of Pittsburgh* murals by the local artist John White Alexander, an allegorical celebration of our industrial city. Its central panel is *The Crowning of Labor*, in which a figure in full plate armor is offered a wreath. In the uppermost story, a public gathering in the park seems to have attracted respectable working class people. (Carnegie Library of Pittsburgh.)

The Hall of Architecture contains plaster casts of extraordinary variety, including a cast of the western doorways of a church at Saint Gilles-du-Gard in France that was one of the largest casts ever made. It serves every Christmas as the background for an antique Neapolitan crèche. (Pittsburgh History & Landmarks Foundation.)

The Hall of Paleontology, or Dinosaur Hall, reflects a Carnegie interest. Indeed, Andrew Carnegie gave the Museum of Natural History a stipend for field work, and one of its displays is a *Diplodocus carnegii*. This photograph shows Dinosaur Hall in its original state. (Carnegie Library of Pittsburgh.)

A humble servant of the Carnegie Institute building and other Civic Center buildings is the Bellefield Boiler Plant, which has stood in Junction Hollow since 1907. It is shown here as enlarged in the 1940s. (Pittsburgh History & Landmarks Foundation.)

Steam from the Bellefield Boiler Plant powered these Corliss engines in the new Carnegie Institute dynamo room. (Carnegie Library of Pittsburgh.)

48

Here is a scene of 1911, with fashionably dressed women leaving the Music Hall after an Easter service. Johann Sebastian Bach looks on, gravely approving. Bellefield Avenue still presents a range of billboards to Forbes Street and Frick Acres, and the houses behind it still belong to Dithridge's old East Pittsburgh development. It will be 15 years before the palatial-looking Pittsburgh Board of Education building opens on the site. (Carnegie Library of Pittsburgh.)

Around 1915, the Associated Artists of Pittsburgh pose on the steps of the Carnegie Library of Pittsburgh Lecture Hall, close to the Schenley Bridge. They have just finished a buffet supper and are soon to attend a lecture. (Carnegie Library of Pittsburgh.)

St. Pierre Ravine, though picturesque and crossed by a handsome stone bridge, was destined not to survive as a City Beautiful feature. Fill from a large public-works project was hauled to the ravine around 1913, and a competition for a new grand entrance to Schenley Park resulted in Schenley Plaza where the ravine had been. Sellers & Register, Philadelphia architects, won the competition. Here it is in 1936, before rows of plane trees were planted in front of the Carnegie Library of Pittsburgh and before Schenley Plaza became a parking lot until its redesign in 2005. Angling off to the upper left is the Schenley Bridge, heading for Flagstaff Hill and Phipps Conservatory. (Pittsburgh City Photographer Collection, Archives Service Center, University of Pittsburgh.)

Five

Carnegie Institute of Technology

In 1904, Andrew Carnegie held a competition for the design of a large school that was to give the children of Pittsburgh the chance for technical educations. The Carnegie Institute and the Carnegie Library of Pittsburgh offered a varied diet for the mind, but Carnegie's original conception of the Carnegie Technical Schools was strictly utilitarian.

He did not know, though, the personality of Henry Hornbostel, the New York architect who won the competition. Hornbostel was a Paris-trained architect of vigor, self-confidence, and imagination, a man who thought big and had a genial, compelling way that eventually reconciled Carnegie to a school that taught the fine arts as well as the useful ones.

In 1912 the Carnegie Technical Schools were renamed the Carnegie Institute of Technology ("Carnegie Tech"), and after a merger with the Mellon Institute of Industrial Research in the 1960s became Carnegie Mellon University.

The master plan and its details evolved, changed form in surprising ways, became less fussy, bolder, and more refined in a gradual process that took nearly a decade for even the main campus to assume its ultimate though incomplete form. One concept, that of a great central lawn, remained: an echo it may be of Thomas Jefferson's University of Virginia, or the recent Columbia University campus. But its terminal features took years to take shape: Machinery Hall, overlooking Junction Hollow, became a dominating mass and raised a chimney at the end of the main axis, surrounded by a circular arcade that Hornbostel termed a temple of Venus. The other end was eventually blocked by a lavish arts building, at first called the School of Applied Design, that celebrated architecture and the other arts literally from floor to ceiling in its public spaces.

The nature of the commission prompted Hornbostel to stress technology as a compositional theme: to execute the main buildings in Kittanning brick, a white industrial material that he ornamented with white and polychromed terra cotta. Inside the technology buildings Hornbostel used sconces and railings of pipe, and vaulted some interiors with Guastavino tile, fashionable then for covering monumental spaces, but here left exposed and raw, in its natural reddish-brown state.

Here we introduce, formally, Henry Hornbostel (1867–1961), whom we glimpsed beside his Westinghouse Memorial. He was a legendary architect of his time, a man who loved to enter competitions, and who won many of them. He was a man who brought a fresh approach to the classical and other styles he might choose, making them modern and American. He will return repeatedly in these pages. (Carnegie Mellon University Archives.)

This is the first master plan for the Carnegie Technical Schools. The left end is that toward Junction Hollow, with a chimney already on axis but with no emphatic structural masses at its side. At the other end, where the School of Applied Design would end up, is a much larger and more complicated multipurpose wing. The diagonal quadrangle at this end was never built. (Pittsburgh History & Landmarks Foundation.)

52

This is the extent to which Hornbostel's ultimate plans were realized. In the foreground, overlooking Junction Hollow, is Machinery Hall, later renamed after Arthur Hamerschlag, the first Superintendent. At the far end is the School of Applied Design, later renamed the College of Fine Arts. To its left is the Margaret Morrison Carnegie School for Women. (Pittsburgh History & Landmarks Foundation.)

Andrew Carnegie and Henry Hornbostel confer on the site, around 1910. (Carnegie Mellon University Archives.)

The theater in the School of Applied Design was rationalized to Andrew Carnegie as an "assembly hall." However, the leaded-glass ceiling, the wall decorations, and the legend over the proscenium—*IÇI L'INSPIRATION DEPLOYE SES AILES* (Here, inspiration unfolds its wings)—hinted at other things. (Carnegie Mellon University Archives.)

This is a drawing class in the School of Applied Design basement in the 1920s. At least one Pittsburgh artist has admitted that she took such classes because women were permitted to smoke there. (Carnegie Mellon University Archives.)

Not far behind the School of Applied Design was the Margaret Morrison Carnegie School for Women, used mainly for training in secretarial work, household economics, and costume design. An inscription around its oval entrance arcade reads, "To make and inspire the home; to lessen suffering and increase happiness; to aid mankind in its upward struggles; to ennoble and adorn life's work, however humble: these are women's high prerogatives." (Pittsburgh History & Landmarks Foundation; courtesy of Stanley Karas.)

Acquired by Carnegie Mellon University in modern times was this nearby building, also by Hornbostel, that had been built in 1917 for the United States Bureau of Mines. Its light, open character with jutting hipped roofs suggests the kind of building the U.S. government was putting up in the Panama Canal Zone and the Philippines at the time, but the cast-concrete portal is a touch of vivid Hornbostelian pomp. (Pittsburgh History & Landmarks Foundation.)

The University of Pittsburgh's Cathedral of Learning and the Schenley Memorial Fountain form, together, a popular symbol of Oakland's role as a municipal showplace. The Cathedral of Learning has a story that requires further exploration, but the fountain's story is more quickly told. When Schenley Plaza was made, the Bellefield Bridge was simply buried, and its axial position suggested its use as a base for a monument to Mary Schenley. Assuming the form of a fountain, this was completed in 1918. The sculptor here was a New Yorker, Victor David Brenner, and the architect was another New Yorker, Harold Van Buren Magonigle. The sculpture is called *A Song to Nature*, and an inscription reads, "Pan the Earth God answers to the magic notes sung to the lyre by sweet Harmony." (Carnegie Library of Pittsburgh.)

Six

PITTSBURGH'S SHOWPLACE

Schenley Park and Andrew Carnegie's cultural palace for the people were remarkable features in 1895 for a neighborhood that was half suburban and residential, and half rural and withdrawn from the city growing around it. But Manifest Destiny was in the air.

In the late 1890s, Franklin Felix Nicola (1859–1938) formed the Bellefield Company, with Andrew Carnegie, Henry J. Heinz, Henry Clay Frick, and Andrew Mellon among his associates. They bought three acres of cornfield from Mary Schenley and there built the Bellefield Hotel. It was quickly renamed the Hotel Schenley, which was opened in 1898. Set in landscaped grounds and close to the Carnegie Library and Schenley Park, this was at once the most glamorous hotel in Pittsburgh.

Nicola's acquisitions of land from the Schenley and O'Hara estates after Mary Schenley's death in 1903 did not provide building sites for absolutely everything in the glamorous quarter that was coming to be, but for almost everything. Nicola's new Schenley Farms Company, formed again with very solid associates, bought and sold land from 1905 on for clubs, institutions (including an entire new plant for the University of Pittsburgh), and for homes in a model neighborhood. His developments were transfixed by another Edward Bigelow project, Grant Boulevard (later, Bigelow Boulevard), winding its way around Herron Hill above the Allegheny, then making its way from the north and cannibalizing the existing street pattern—where there was any—to go past the model homes and clubhouses to the place where Schenley Plaza would come to be. (In our hilly city we never succeeded in getting a grand axial avenue with look-alike institutional buildings symmetrically disposed: just as well.)

Most of the Oakland Civic Center and adjacent City Beautiful properties appear in this view from 1954. Left of Fifth Avenue are, from the bottom to the top, University Place, the Soldiers' Memorial (now the Soldiers & Sailors National Military Museum and Memorial) with its great lawn, the Syria Mosque, the old University Club, and at the corner, the Pittsburgh Athletic Association, with the Masonic Temple just up the street. To their left, almost wholly unseen, is the Schenley Farms residential area. Across Fifth Avenue from the Soldiers' Memorial are the Hotel Schenley and the five-unit Schenley Apartments, and across Bigelow Boulevard from that, the Cathedral of Learning with the attendant Stephen Foster Memorial and Heinz Chapel. Near the Fifth Avenue bend, where the soot-blackened Bellefield Presbyterian Church stands, comes Bellefield Avenue, with the colonnaded Mellon Institute, the Young Men and Women's Hebrew Association, and the Pittsburgh Board of Education side by side. Beyond them is St. Paul's Cathedral. Forbes Street diverges from Fifth Avenue at the right, with Schenley Plaza, the Carnegie Library of Pittsburgh and Carnegie Institute, and—across Junction Hollow—the Carnegie Institute of Technology, with Schenley Park to the far right. (Carnegie Library of Pittsburgh.)

This view from around 1900 shows the Oakland Civic Center land. To the right is the Hotel Schenley. In the distance are the Carnegie Library and Schenley Park. Along Fifth Avenue at the left, the houses of Casey's Row await their fate, unsuspecting. In the foreground, St. Pierre Street, soon to be converted into Grant Boulevard, straggles southward. In the foreground, cows graze where the University of Pittsburgh is to rise. (Carnegie Library of Pittsburgh.)

This 1916 postcard obligingly catalogues the Oakland Civic Center progress to date. (Pittsburgh History & Landmarks Foundation.)

The Hotel Schenley and its neighbors looked like this from the Pittsburgh Athletic Association around 1920. A temporary concert hall extends from the hotel toward Bigelow Boulevard. To the rear at the left are Schenley Plaza and Forbes Field, and to the right, the Oakland Methodist Episcopal Church, which had been there since 1874. (Carnegie Library of Pittsburgh.)

Here is a meeting in the Schenley ballroom, held by the Carnegie Company in 1901, possibly as part of the formation of United States Steel. (The Historical Society of Western Pennsylvania.)

In this picture from around 1930, the Hotel Schenley stands in its ample grounds with the Schenley Apartments behind. To the left are fragments of Forbes Field and the Schenley Theatre, a movie house. Architects for the Hotel Schenley had been Rutan & Russell, a prominent local firm. Henry Hornbostel (who had designed both the Schenley Theatre façade and the Soldiers' Memorial) collaborated with Rutan & Russell and Eric Fisher Wood on the Schenley Apartments; he lived there himself. (Pittsburgh History & Landmarks Foundation.)

This rendering, from a rental booklet in 1922, shows the Forbes Street entrance to the Schenley Apartments courtyard. (Pittsburgh History & Landmarks Foundation.)

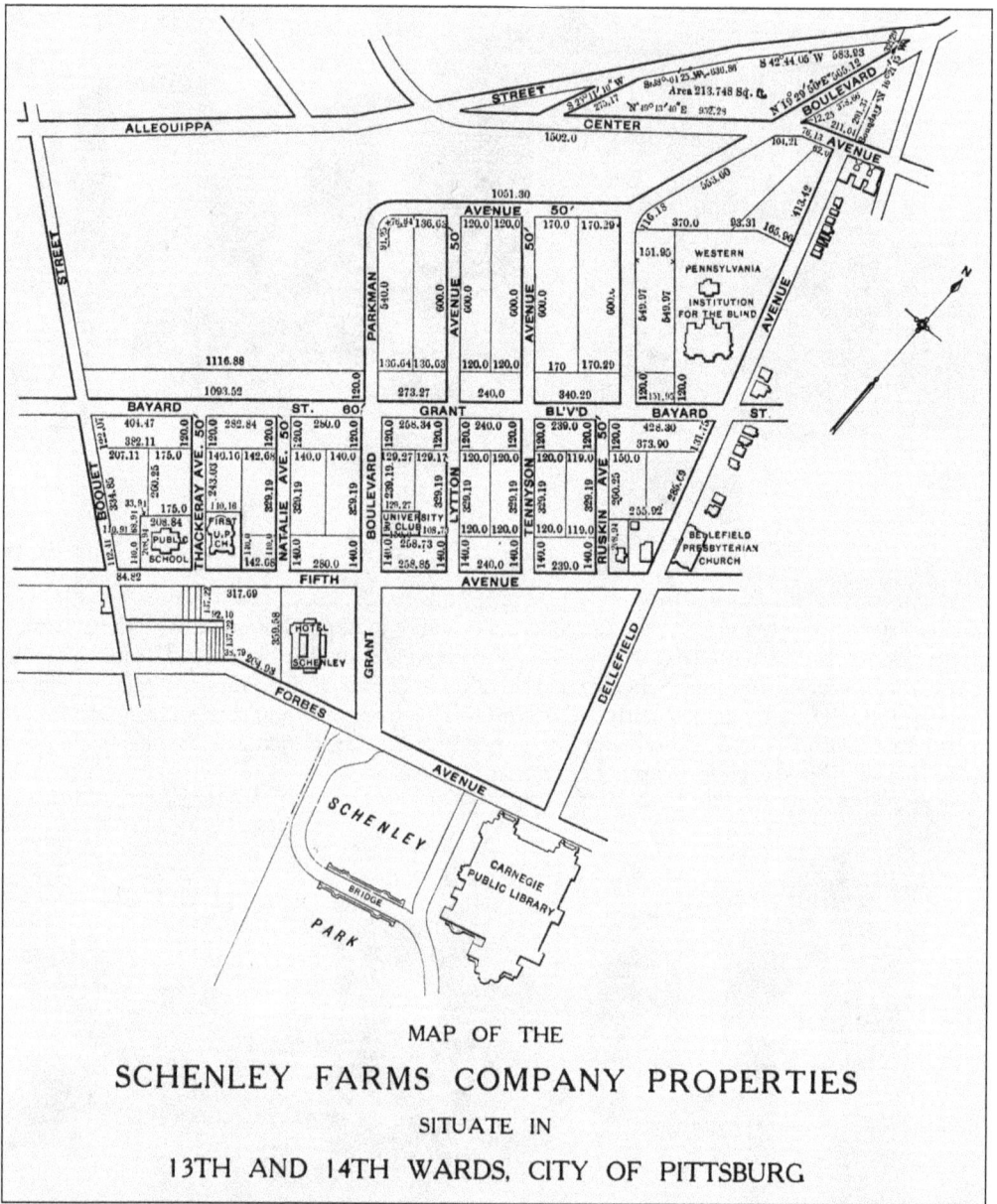

MAP OF THE

SCHENLEY FARMS COMPANY PROPERTIES

SITUATE IN

13TH AND 14TH WARDS, CITY OF PITTSBURG

Here are the Schenley Farms holdings around 1906. A few features are notable. First, notice how Grant (later Bigelow) Boulevard enters diagonally from the north, heads southeast, turns southwest and appropriates three blocks of a street that is also called Bayard, then heads southeastward on a continuation of Parkman Avenue. The residential area of Schenley Farms lies between Grant and Allequippa. The area between Parkman and Bouquet will be sold to the University of Pittsburgh for its new campus, and the area between Bayard (or Grant) and Fifth is intended for the Oakland Civic Center; several buildings, old and new, are already up. To further the complication of street names, Bayard along the University of Pittsburgh property will actually be called O'Hara Street. (Carnegie Library of Pittsburgh.)

An early arrival in this new Oakland, in the Bellefield area at Fifth and Craig, was St. Paul's Roman Catholic Cathedral. The old downtown cathedral property had been bought by Henry Clay Frick for one of his real-estate ventures, and the diocese built this new church in one of the city's up-and-coming neighborhoods; it opened in 1906. The architects were Egan & Prindeville, of Chicago. (Carnegie Library of Pittsburgh.)

The brilliant local architect Edward Joseph Weber designed Central Catholic High School around the corner on Fifth Avenue, which opened in 1927. Weber's use of brickwork, strawberry-colored with inlaid patterns of black, was almost mid-Victorian in its boldness. (Pittsburgh History & Landmarks Foundation.)

Bird's-Eye View of the Plaza as It Would Look if It Were Made.

The expression "City Beautiful," fashionable as a concept at the turn of the century, was being used with regard to Oakland by 1904. In this newspaper sketch, the Hotel Schenley is to the far left and St. Paul's Cathedral to the far right, with the Bellefield Presbyterian Church to its left. The Carnegie Institute and Carnegie Library of Pittsburgh are to the lower left. Fifth Avenue, Forbes Street, Bellefield Avenue, and Craig Street actually existed, but all other buildings and streets are imaginary. (Carnegie Library of Pittsburgh.)

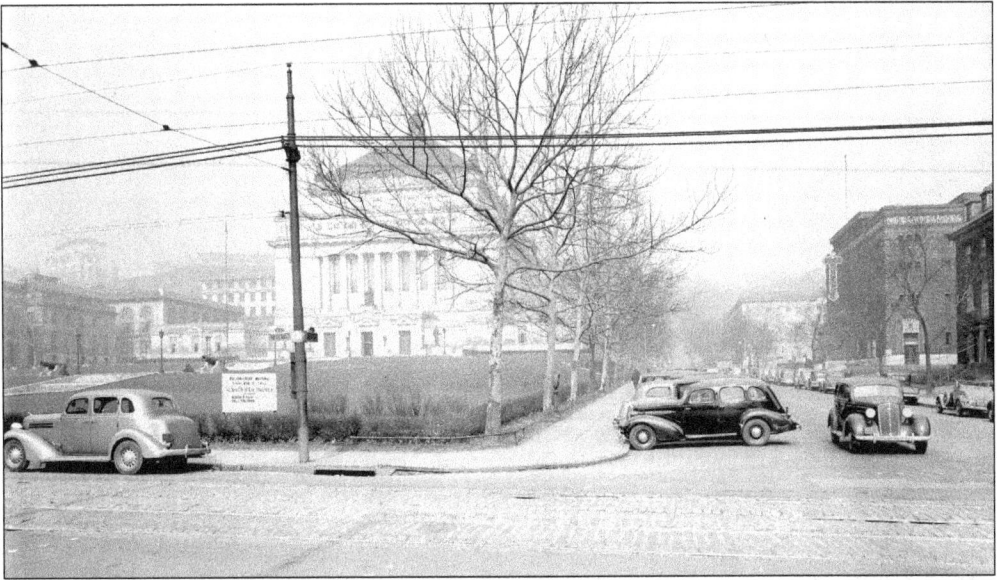

In 1906, Henry Hornbostel, already busy in Oakland, found time to enter the competition for the Allegheny County Soldiers' Memorial, a Civil War commemorative building. It was intended to face onto Grant Boulevard but in execution was rotated to face down a great lawn toward the Hotel Schenley. This March 1937 view from Fifth Avenue, looking up Bigelow Boulevard, shows the Soldiers' Memorial to the left. (Pittsburgh City Photographer Collection, Archives Service Center, University of Pittsburgh.)

This is the interior of the Soldiers' Memorial auditorium, used among other things for commencements and Pittsburgh Symphony Orchestra recording sessions. Behind the platform, the Gettysburg Address is boldly inscribed in the wall. The building also has a banquet room, two meeting rooms, and a military museum. (Carnegie Library of Pittsburgh.)

In this scene from around 1910 we are looking from the Hotel Schenley toward the Pittsburgh Athletic Association (PAA), a work by the new firm of Janssen & Abbott, who were about to become Pittsburgh's outstanding society architects. The architecture is Venetian Renaissance. To its left, up Grant (or Bigelow) Boulevard, is the University Club of 1905 by MacClure & Spahr, a local office that had a thriving business and residential practice. Behind the two clubhouses, Nicola's model residential development Schenley Farms is beginning to be built up. Right of the PAA is the Fifth Avenue lot where the Masonic Temple will soon rise, and in the far right background it looks as if work is starting on the First Baptist Church. The lawn corner to the lower left belongs to the Soldiers' Memorial, and that to the right, to Frick Acres, where the Cathedral of Learning will dominate the whole scene in a couple of decades. On the skyline are houses of the Upper Hill, a different and by now old neighborhood, beyond the former Schenley holdings. (Pittsburgh History & Landmarks Foundation.)

Beyond the 1905 University Club, on Bigelow Boulevard, was the Syria Temple (or Syria Mosque) that was constructed in 1915. Built for the Shriners, it was also, for many years, successor to the Carnegie Institute Music Hall as the auditorium for the Pittsburgh Symphony Orchestra (PSO). It was designed by Huehl, Holmes & Schmidt of Chicago: its striped quasi-Arabic treatment led to its comparison to a large mocha torte. It came down in 1991 despite great protest. (Pittsburgh History & Landmarks Foundation.)

This is the Syria Mosque auditorium during a concert. (Carnegie Library of Pittsburgh.)

The Masonic Temple was built by Janssen & Abbott. Despite normal-sized windows on the ground floor, there is enough wall area, and the entrance doorways are tall enough, to give an arcane effect quite in contrast to the open, lavish geniality of the Pittsburgh Athletic Association next door. The lower two floors are treated as a massive, projecting podium on which a temple rises. This construction photograph dates from August 26, 1914. (University Archives, University of Pittsburgh.)

The Webster Hall hotel, which opened in 1926, stands on Fifth Avenue between the Bellefield Presbyterian Church and St. Paul's Cathedral. Here it is in a photograph from the 1950s. The front is more or less Byzantine, but at the time the rooms inside were French, Spanish, Tudor, Georgian, and "Victorian." (Pittsburgh History & Landmarks Foundation.)

The Oakland Civic Center was a work of the Eclectic period in American architecture, when the style of a building often alluded to the past of the cultural institution it housed. Thus, the Mellon Institute was Greek Ionic because in Greece much of science originated, while St. Paul's was Gothic, a style associated with Christianity. The Webster Hall hotel was less principled in its vague Byzantine manner. We have already seen the Pittsburgh Athletic Association, open and worldly Venetian; the Masonic Temple, with an ancient, closed, secretive look; and the mock-Islamic Syria Mosque. (Carnegie Library of Pittsburgh.)

Here is the Mellon Institute itself—designed by Janssen's later partnership, Janssen & Cocken—as seen from Webster Hall in the 1950s. Inside the colonnade—which is pure display, a coolly extravagant architectural gesture—is a stripped classical reception hall, a Carolean library with woodwork in the manner of Grinling Gibbons, and nine floors of research laboratories, three of them underground. (University Archives, University of Pittsburgh.)

The Mellon Institute colonnade is surrounded by 62 unfluted Ionic columns, 42 feet high, whose 36-foot shafts are 60-ton limestone monoliths that were quarried and turned in Indiana, brought here by rail, hauled over specially reinforced streets, and set up as shown here. (Carnegie Library of Pittsburgh.)

Next door to the Mellon Institute on Bellefield Avenue, after 1924, was the Young Men and Women's Hebrew Association building by Benno Janssen: a truly eclectic building, stylistically free, suggesting a palazzo perhaps because of its great rusticated archway but in fact alluding to no specific function or national idiom. Janssen used this combination of bold rusticated stone archway and dark red brick in at least two other instances. (University Archives, University of Pittsburgh.)

The palatial Pittsburgh Board of Education building, completed in 1926, was the work of Ingham & Boyd, architects of institutional buildings and mansions. Their work seldom thrilled but always pleased. The Easter scene from 1911 outside the Carnegie Institute Music Hall (on page 49) shows the raw spread of billboards and old wooden houses that this serene façade replaced. (The Historical Society of Western Pennsylvania.)

71

In 1923, the University Club opened a new building on Natalie Avenue (later, University Place), across the Soldiers' Memorial lawn from its old home. It was a work by Henry Hornbostel. Its proudest interior is an Adam-style dining room in the upper floor of the wing that juts toward the street. Its roof terrace has a remarkable view of the Oakland Civic Center. (Pittsburgh History & Landmarks Foundation.)

Up University Place from the new University Club was the Concordia Club, a social club which had moved there from the North Side around 1913. (Pittsburgh History & Landmarks Foundation.)

At the head of University Place is O'Hara Street, seen here in 1914 (although, actually, the nearest stretch has been commandeered by Bigelow Boulevard, in its devious course, as far as the corner). The nearest building is the Historical Society of Western Pennsylvania, by Ingham & Boyd, built in 1912. Next to it is the Twentieth Century Club, as first built in 1910. These two buildings are just within the boundaries of Nicola's Schenley Farms residential district. Beyond them is the abortive hillside campus of the University of Pittsburgh, with Engineering Hall at street level and, at the top of the hill, what was built of the School of Medicine: both by Henry Hornbostel. (Courtesy of Mary A. McDonough.)

Across O'Hara Street from the University of Pittsburgh, Nicola sold property to the Central Turnverein, a German-American gymnastic club that opened its new building in 1912. The architects were Kiehnel & Elliott, a local office whose mildly progressive work sometimes, as here, reflected what was happening around Chicago at the time. The building has been owned by the University of Pittsburgh since 1920, when it was bought for a dental clinic. (Pittsburgh History & Landmarks Foundation.)

Facing the Turnverein across Thackeray Street was the Gen. Albert J. Logan Armory, built in 1911. The stone street fronts by the W. G. Wilkins Company were most impressive, but pupils of the neighboring Frick School got to see only rear walls of bare brick. (Carnegie Library of Pittsburgh.)

At the corner of Bigelow Boulevard and Parkman Avenue, a progressive women's organization, the Twentieth Century Club, built this modest structure in 1910. The architect was a local man, George H. Schwan. Two of the Schenley Farms houses can be seen to the right. (Carnegie Library of Pittsburgh.)

In 1929 the size of the club was doubled, and an entirely new façade was given to the building. The architects this time were Janssen & Cocken. (Pittsburgh History & Landmarks Foundation.)

At Bellefield Avenue and Bayard Street (which later, please recall, is O'Hara Street, alias Bigelow Boulevard, under yet a third name) is the First Baptist Church, a masterly work of the New York architect Bertram Grosvenor Goodhue. Completed in 1912, its Gothic style is sometimes delicate but never fussy, and its detailing subtle: surely one of the best thought out buildings in the city. Even the jointing of its random-ashlar stonework, almost invisible, is artfully composed. (Pittsburgh History & Landmarks Foundation.)

Goodhue had to adapt Gothic architecture to a denomination that is centered on adult baptism. He gave the baptistery prominence behind the altar and under the great organ case in his highly effective interior. The vaults are among the first built of Akoustolith, a ceramic tile developed by the Guastavino Company, to suppress echoes. (Pittsburgh History & Landmarks Foundation.)

If we think of Oakland as a showplace, we should consider the performing facilities that attracted people from all over the region. The Schenley Theatre, a movie house of 1914, may be marginal in this regard, despite its proximity to the Hotel Schenley (whose portico is at the right). Its façade (not the remainder of the building) is by the ubiquitous Henry Hornbostel. (Courtesy of Mary A. McDonough.)

The Casino that stood in Schenley Park beside Junction Hollow had only a few years to establish itself as the highly popular hockey and ice-skating rink it was before being destroyed, in 1896, by a fire that also ruined the first Schenley Bridge. (Carnegie Library of Pittsburgh.)

The loss of the Schenley Park Casino led to the adaptation of the recently vacated Duquesne Traction Company trolley barn, on Craig Street just north of Fifth Avenue, as an arena that was called at various times the Duquesne Garden, the Duquesne Gardens, or toward the last, simply The Gardens. This view shows it shortly after its opening in 1899. (Carnegie Library of Pittsburgh.)

The Gardens, shown here toward the end, had a large and adaptable space with surprisingly good acoustics. It accommodated ice hockey, ice skating, roller skating, tennis, boxing, and even opera. Schumann-Heink and Caruso sang there, and Victor Herbert and John Philip Sousa conducted there. It came down in 1956, along with Isaac Hobbs's 1870s-period A. A. Carrier villa next door. (The Historical Society of Western Pennsylvania.)

After 1909, Forbes Field was an unlikely neighbor of the Schenley Hotel and the Carnegie Library of Pittsburgh, which it faced across St. Pierre Ravine and later across Schenley Plaza. It was Pittsburgh's baseball stadium through the 1970 season, successor to Exposition Park on the city's North Side. This view is from about 1910, with St. Pierre Ravine and the Bellefield Bridge in the middle distance. (Carnegie Library of Pittsburgh.)

Here is a view from the Cathedral of Learning of Forbes Field with the old Linden Grove area beyond it, and beyond that, nearly a mile away and 150 feet below, heavy industry by the Monongahela River. (Pittsburgh History & Landmarks Foundation.)

79

Luna Park existed briefly on North Craig Street at the start of Baum Boulevard. In name and conception it imitated a popular new attraction at Coney Island. No trace remains of Luna Park, which lasted only from 1904 to 1909; even the buildings that replaced it are gone or unrecognizable. (Carnegie Library of Pittsburgh.)

Luna Park's architectural effects owed debts to China, Venice, and various Hispanic and Islamic cultures; the happy promiscuity of styles in the Oakland Civic Center was here carried to an extreme. (Carnegie Library of Pittsburgh.)

Seven

SCHENLEY FARMS

It may seem strange that Franklin Nicola chose to plan a residential area in 1905 in a part of the Schenley property that was hemmed in to the north by hilly ground, to the south by at least the promise of monumental buildings, to the west by the bare ground he may have already had in mind for the University of Pittsburgh, and only to the east by an established residential neighborhood—and not much shopping anywhere near by. But he did. Along with the more public buildings on the old Schenley property, Nicola had 3½ blocks laid out for residential use, each 600 feet long and about half as wide, bounded by avenues named after authors—Parkman, Lytton, and Tennyson—as well as portions of Grant, or Bigelow, Boulevard. The development extended northward, too, beyond the existing Centre Avenue to include the new Schenley Farms Terrace. Around the time when all this was laid out, there was talk of construction of one or more subway lines, which would have stations a quarter mile away and would afford a quick ride from downtown. The automobile was becoming a reality, too, in the lives of the Pittsburghers who would settle in Schenley Farms.

To show the upper-middle-class standard of housing he had in mind, Nicola built 12 houses along Lytton Avenue, as technologically advanced as houses could be at the time. There were gas-*and*-electric lighting fixtures, just in case; "refrigerators" still dependent on the iceman; and the central vacuum-cleaning systems that were technologically chic. One important feature, in those days before municipal water filtration, was a charcoal filter for each house. The streets were planted with plane trees, had Manhattan-type lampposts, and—very unusual for Pittsburgh then, and even later—all wiring was underground. J. W. W. Elliott, "the well-known landscaper," had terraced and planted the lots in a unified scheme.

Over the next quarter century, 129 houses were built in a variety of styles: Craftsman, Tudor, English Rustic, and a little Renaissance, for the most part. They shared the area with the Twentieth Century Club and the Historical Society of Western Pennsylvania, but not with churches at first, and never with commerce.

A few pictures published in 1914 in two issues of *The Builder* show Schenley Farms in its earliest days, not fully built up yet. The First Baptist Church is just outside the development, on the other side of Bayard Street. The Arts and Crafts house stands on Bigelow Boulevard, awaiting its neighbor—the grandiose Italianate villa we will see on page 86. (Courtesy of Mary A. McDonough.)

A view of Schenley Farms from the elevation of Fairfield Lane. Parkman Avenue, in the foreground, is little occupied thus far, but some houses have gone up on Bigelow Boulevard. In the distance, left to right, are the Western Pennsylvania Institution for the Blind; Rodef Shalom Temple, far off in Shadyside; St. Paul's Cathedral; the First Baptist Church; and the Bellefield Presbyterian Church. (Courtesy of Mary A. McDonough.)

Here is another view toward the Oakland Civic Center from Fairfield Lane, looking along Lytton Avenue, with the rear of the Pittsburgh Athletic Association prominent on the left, and the still-rugged hillside campus for the University of Pittsburgh on the right. (Courtesy of Mary A. McDonough.)

These were the 12 houses on Lytton Avenue built by Nicola as demonstrations of the type of dwelling expected in Schenley Farms. In the foreground is one of his New York–type lampposts. (Courtesy of Mary A. McDonough.)

The massive retaining wall along Parkman Avenue becomes evident at the corner where Parkman turns southward toward the Oakland Civic Center. The steps lead to Fairfield Lane, which runs parallel to Parkman and Centre Avenues. (Courtesy of Mary A. McDonough.)

This Arts and Crafts house on Tennyson Avenue is a little unusual in its high-waisted look, a stuccoed second floor above high walls of rock-faced random ashlar. In the next picture, we see this house in its setting. (Courtesy of Mary A. McDonough.)

This is a northerly view up Tennyson Avenue toward Parkman, with Centre Avenue houses on the skyline. The mixture of Tudor with Arts and Crafts is typical for 1914. (Courtesy of Mary A. McDonough.)

The Godfrey Stengel House, dating from 1913, was an especially handsome Arts and Crafts building. It was by Kiehnel & Elliott, the architects for the Central Turnverein a few blocks away. Apart from the tabernacle on the second-floor front it has no special stylistic allusions, relying on the perceived mass, the color, the texture, and the patterning of brickwork for effect. (Pittsburgh History & Landmarks Foundation.)

Around 1915 Louis Stevens created this limestone house, half palazzo, half villa, with an evocation of Renaissance Italy clearly in mind. It stands at the corner where Bigelow Boulevard, having made its way from the north through Schenley Farms, turns southwestward along its southern border. First Baptist Church is across the street. The griffins by the front door were salvaged from the Lewis Block, a Victorian office building downtown. (Pittsburgh History & Landmarks Foundation.)

Driveways are not much in evidence in early photographs of Schenley Farms, and it is interesting to see this 1912 design for a parking garage proposed to serve the development. The situation suggests a chauffeur to collect the car, crank it into life, and call at the house to take the man of the house to work or the lady for shopping. The designers were the W. G. Wilkins Company. (Pittsburgh History & Landmarks Foundation.)

Eight

THE UNIVERSITY
OF PITTSBURGH

As if continuing to refine and execute the designs for the Carnegie Institute of Technology, teaching an architectural course at Carnegie Tech, realizing his design for the Soldiers' Memorial, and engaging in major projects outside the city were not enough, Henry Hornbostel entered a master plan in a 1908 competition for a whole new campus for the Western University of Pennsylvania (which was almost immediately renamed the University of Pittsburgh).

He won against 60 competitors and achieved, perhaps, a unique experience: the task of realizing two university-sized institutions within a mile of each other. Forty-three acres of Schenley hillside pastureland were to be converted into a gigantic, close-built Acropolis, 1,000 feet deep and 250 feet high. In the event, little was built. Ambition exceeded means, and the site proved in places to be unreliable because of worked-out coal mines, some of which, in fact, were burning.

John Gabbert Bowman (1888–1962) came to the University of Pittsburgh as chancellor in 1921, at the age of 43. He had been director of the American College of Surgeons, and had had other medical school experience. At Pittsburgh, his new "plant" consisted of five Hornbostel buildings, the new Alumni Hall by Janssen & Abbott (whose placement had wrecked Hornbostel's grand plan), and a few temporary buildings left over from the recent war. But Bowman was one of history's great persuaders, and in 1926 work began on an academic skyscraper then unique as a type—London and Moscow universities came later—on Frick Acres. Bowman had persuaded R. B. and Andrew Mellon to buy the 14 acres of prime land and give it to the university. He had visited with Charles Zeller Klauder, a Philadelphia architect who specialized in academic work, and had at last got him to design this "Cathedral of Learning," Gothic and with masses leaping above masses, after an emotional creative session during which Bowman and Klauder were inspired by the Magic Fire Music from Richard Wagner's *Walküre.*

The Cathedral of Learning, 535 feet high, was not very practical as an academic building—think of class changes by elevator—but it was intended as inspirational. Like the Carnegie Library 300 yards away, it was intended to draw the young toward better lives. It was to express "courage and spirituality . . . a powerful note of victory and adventure." The Cathedral of Learning certainly gave the Oakland Civic Center a focus and signaled its presence to people far away. Later, two other buildings came to Frick Acres: the nondenominational Heinz Memorial Chapel and the Stephen Foster Memorial, with its museum and theaters.

This is Henry Hornbostel's rendered elevation submitted in the competition of 1908. A giant escalator was to run from bottom to top. The individual building designs that were executed were altered by Hornbostel into bolder and more original works than those shown on this elevation. As with Carnegie Tech, Hornbostel won the commission, then apparently relaxed and proceeded

to put in his best efforts on the details. The composition as a whole would have been seen most clearly and completely from the Carnegie Tech campus; Hornbostel may have intended this. (Pittsburgh History & Landmarks Foundation.)

As the design evolved, the main entrance at O'Hara Street (left) and Parkman Avenue (right) was projected to look like this. The temple-like central building on the main axis was never executed. The School of Engineering is to the left, the School of Mines to the right. (Pittsburgh History & Landmarks Foundation.)

This is a view from 1924 of the School of Engineering, which was never quite completed. In Hornbostel's executed design, the lower two floors form a jutting, simple base on which the temple-like upper floors, with their lavish terra-cotta detailing, are raised. Down O'Hara Street is the Mellon Institute of Industrial Research, a building from 1915 that harmonized with Hornbostel's buildings, but was not one of them. (Carnegie Library of Pittsburgh.)

As with its mate the School of Engineering, the School of Mines was never completed and is now gone. On the skyline is the little that was executed of the Medical School. (Pittsburgh History & Landmarks Foundation.)

The Medical School as proposed would have been a handsome composition following the curve of a hillside drive, with its library as a prominent feature, as this sketch of 1913 illustrates. (Pittsburgh History & Landmarks Foundation.)

A rendering from 1910 shows the completed Medical School's entrance front. (Pittsburgh History & Landmarks Foundation.)

This much was actually finished by early 1913. Charles Keck's terra-cotta figure of *Aesculapius*, the ancient medical god, overlooked Oakland for nine decades, then was put in storage when the building came down. (Carnegie Library of Pittsburgh.)

Here we see the University of Pittsburgh campus and some neighbors between 1915 and 1920. In the foreground, this side of O'Hara Street, are the Central Turnverein and the Concordia Club. Across the street are the Mellon Institute and the School of Engineering, with the Medical and Dental Schools uphill. Alumni Hall and Pitt Stadium would soon be built. (University Archives, University of Pittsburgh.)

Pitt Stadium was a poured-concrete oval, 791 feet by 617 feet, built in 1925 by enthusiastic alumni rather than by the struggling university. It had a capacity of 67,000, and could have been enlarged to accommodate 30,000 more. It had a stately, simple beauty, and was the design of W. S. Hindman, a Pitt alumnus. (Carnegie Library of Pittsburgh.)

This view from the early 1950s shows the way in which the stadium's huge oval nestled into the hillside. The great gateway facing down DeSoto Street is to the right. At the top of the photograph, the Veterans' Hospital is being framed up. (Allegheny Conference on Community Development, The Historical Society of Western Pennsylvania.)

Frick Acres is seen here from the Hotel Schenley around 1920. The Browne House is in the foreground. A well-known Pittsburgh architect, Edward B. Lee, had lived in this house and composed a picture with this house and the frame of the Cathedral of Learning superimposed. A family member recalled, "Near Forbes Street . . . was a little brook that meandered through a cornfield; kids could find crayfish in it and splash stones in its pools." (University Archives, University of Pittsburgh.)

Around 1930, the Cathedral of Learning is framed up and further work is proceeding. The basic structure of the tower, it has been estimated, will last 300 years. The heavy steelwork is coated in pine pitch, encased in a foot of concrete, and then faced in limestone. Subsequent university buildings, in the meantime, will presumably come and go. The view is from Bigelow Boulevard. (Carnegie Library of Pittsburgh.)

The Cathedral of Learning and the attendant Heinz Chapel appear in a view across Bellefield Avenue, taken around 1940. Some have felt that the Cathedral of Learning looks a little thin seen in elevation, that a view from an angle brings out the real beauty to be found in the rich complexity of the masses, the taper of the tower above its lowest floors. If *Die Walküre* inspired the massing of the Cathedral of Learning, that of the chapel is said to have appeared to Klauder in a dream. (Carnegie Library of Pittsburgh.)

At the heart of the Cathedral of Learning is the Commons Room, 128 feet by 175 feet in area and 52 feet high: an independent masonry structure within the building's steel frame, rising to vaults of stone and Guastavino tile. (University Archives, University of Pittsburgh.)

Screening one entrance to the Commons Room is this grand gate by Samuel Yellin, the renowned Philadelphia ironworker. (Pittsburgh History & Landmarks Foundation.)

An early decision was made to surround the Commons Room with classrooms in the traditional architectural styles of the nations composing the varied ancestries of Pittsburghers. This is one of the Nationality Rooms, that of Sweden. (University Archives, University of Pittsburgh, photographed by H. K. Barnett.)

William Croghan had enlarged Picnic House, a suburban pleasure pavilion of 1835, into a full-size house in the hope of getting Mary Schenley and her husband back, permanently, to the Pittsburgh area. The attempt failed but the house stood until 1946. The decorative work of the ballroom and adjacent rotunda by Philadelphia artist Mordecai Van Horne was reinstalled in the Cathedral of Learning in 1955, though reduced in height. (University Archives, University of Pittsburgh.)

The lavishly detailed Heinz Chapel is in the Flamboyant style of 15th-century France, and includes, in its transept-like side walls, four windows that are 73 feet high and include about 25,000 pieces of stained glass each. The glazier, Charles Connick, had begun his career in Pittsburgh. The chapel is nondenominational, and since its dedication in 1938 has been a favorite wedding and concert location in the Pittsburgh area. (University Archives, University of Pittsburgh.)

The Stephen Foster Memorial is French Flamboyant again, with an auditorium entrance from Forbes Street and an adjacent museum of Foster memorabilia. It was opened in 1937. (Carnegie Library of Pittsburgh.)

The museum of the Foster Memorial takes the polygonal form of a medieval chapter house, an assembly place where the affairs of a cathedral were deliberated. The alcoves are novel features, though, with their miniature archways. (Foster Hall Collection, Center for American Music, University of Pittsburgh Library System.)

Nine

THE MEDICAL CENTER

One element of the present Medical Center, Children's Hospital, already existed as an institution in Oakland at the beginning of the 20th century, occupying an adapted house in the southwestern part of the neighborhood. But the Medical Center began as a project in 1921, when the University of Pittsburgh Medical School was told that unless it developed a closer teaching relationship with local hospitals, it would no longer get a "Class A" rating, and its students would no longer be accredited in Pennsylvania. John Bowman, the new chancellor, had had medical school experience already and was generally aware of the problem. He persuaded the university, despite its lack of cash, to buy the 12-acre H. K. Porter estate at Fifth between Lothrop and DeSoto as a site to which hospitals might relocate.

The Medical School-Medical Center alliance was an idea whose time had come in the 1920s, and its realization followed this sequence: Children's Hospital opened on its new site on the Porter estate in 1927. Montefiore moved down nearby from its Centre Avenue site to what had once been the Eichbaum estate in 1928. Presbyterian, Eye and Ear, and Women's were to be in a unified structure on the Porter estate; this was under contract in 1930. The Falk Clinic opened on the Porter estate in 1931. Opening nearby were the Municipal Hospital and the Western State Psychiatric Hospital, in 1940. Further away, on the Childs-Magee estate The Maples, the Elizabeth Steel Magee Hospital had opened in 1915. There were other medical buildings, and buildings for doctor's offices: most notably among the latter, the Medical Arts Building of 1932 that had replaced a streetcar-line powerhouse at Fifth and Atwood.

The hospitals have continued to expand, and indeed, have architecturally smothered themselves. Children's is moving to a new facility in Lawrenceville, but the others still seem committed to the proximity of Pitt and the steep hillside sites where villas stood a century and a half ago.

This is a newspaper aerial view of the Medical Center around 1950, not long before the Veterans' Hospital was built. (Pittsburgh History & Landmarks Foundation.)

The Children's Hospital on the old H. K. Porter property was opened in 1927. The architects were York & Sawyer, hospital specialists from New York, with collaboration from Edward Purcell Mellon, an architect member of the banking family who also designed the Presbyterian, Eye and Ear, and Women's Hospital building, and the Falk Clinic. (The Historical Society of Western Pennsylvania.)

The earlier Children's Hospital had been at Ophelia and Hamlet Streets in the southwestern part of Oakland since 1890, in a villa-like building that had belonged to John McDevitt. (Pittsburgh History & Landmarks Foundation.)

This is the Falk Clinic, shortly after its opening in 1931. It had been founded in 1928 by the philanthropists Leon and Maurice Falk to serve as a medical and surgical outpatient dispensary, and as part of the University of Pittsburgh's Medical School. (University Archives, University of Pittsburgh.)

The Medical Center institutions that had occupied the Porter property by the mid-1930s are, from left to right, the building that houses the Eye and Ear and the Presbyterian Hospitals (still lacking its right wing for Women's Hospital); the Children's Hospital; and the Falk Clinic. The Western State Psychiatric Hospital is not yet built. In the background are the Pitt Stadium and the Pitt Medical and Dental Schools. (Pittsburgh History & Landmarks Foundation.)

This view from 1939 shows the site of the Municipal Hospital, with the Western State Psychiatric Hospital (Raymond Marlier, 1940), the Cathedral of Learning far away, and the Presbyterian and its companion hospitals in their newly completed building. (Pittsburgh City Photographer Collection, Archives Service Center, University of Pittsburgh.)

The Municipal Hospital was built in 1940 to the design of Richard Irving and Theodore Eicholz. Built as a hospital for contagious diseases, it was the location of Jonas Salk's research for the polio vaccine and is now known as Salk Hall. (The Historical Society of Western Pennsylvania.)

From 1927 on, a grand new Montefiore Hospital occupied a large hillside area in what had been the Third Church Colony, on the site of William Eichbaum's house. This is a view northeastward from Fifth Avenue in 1929. To the far left is the lower end of Chesterfield Road. The mansard-roofed tower of the *c.* 1870 Reilly House is just visible toward the left center. (The Historical Society of Western Pennsylvania.)

Montefiore was a design of Schmidt, Garden & Erikson, a Chicago office, with collaboration from Henry Hornbostel. This view from the 1950s also shows the Catholic school Mount Mercy and the roofs of Chesterfield Road. (The Historical Society of Western Pennsylvania.)

Previously, Montefiore had occupied the S. S. Blackamore House, a Greek Revival villa much remodeled, that stood on Centre Avenue in the Upper Hill. (Pittsburgh History & Landmarks Foundation.)

The Elizabeth Steel Magee Hospital, opened in 1915, occupied the grounds of The Maples, the Magee estate in the southwestern part of Oakland not far from the older Children's Hospital. (The Historical Society of Western Pennsylvania.)

Here is the Medical Center in the early 1950s, with Fifth Avenue passing east to west in the lower left and the Golden Triangle on the skyline to the right. Medical Center buildings are, from left to right, Montefiore Hospital; Falk Clinic, with a large new Nurses' Residence up Lothrop Street next to it; up Lothrop Street from that, the completed Presbyterian, Eye and Ear, and Women's Hospital building; uphill from *that,* the Municipal Hospital; to this side of all these, Children's Hospital; in front of Pitt Stadium, Western State Psychiatric Hospital. Downhill from this last, on Bouquet Street, ground is being cleared for still further construction. (Carnegie Library of Pittsburgh.)

Ten

AN OAKLAND
MISCELLANY

I write of Oakland as one who has been in and out of the area since 1932, one whose reference point is a big, clumsy old house at Fifth and Lothrop, long gone, leaving no trace. A snapshot from around 1940 brings me back: its three stories of porches, rising beyond the two basswood trees on the raised front lawn. In the foreground, a touring car and other bygone vehicles parked on Lothrop Street's Ligonier stone. Beside the house, a big and unruly ailanthus. A house of the old Smoky City among others of its sort, way back when the huckster called with his horse-drawn wagon, the iceman with his tongs and dripping blocks, and now and then the scissors grinder. A place where I found life good: enjoyed the brass-colored evenings, with the cicadas rasping in their insistent, rhythmic way, and the nights that smelled at times of coal smoke, when the Bessemer flares reflected shakily from the clouds, and an occasional whistle sound—the organ tone of a steamboat, the shout of a locomotive—reached us from a mile away and a couple of hundred feet below. Romantic, these phenomena from the age of steam. But I did not have to do the laundry.

The Medical Center was moving in on us in the 1930s, and was destined to swallow us entirely, we of that part of Oakland. For the time being, though, the randomly sited quarters of Dr. Ketterer, Dr. Maddox, Oscar's Turkish Baths, the G. H. Siegal Ironworks, the Betsy Ross Tea Room, and the Ancient Order of Hibernians were secure along Fifth Avenue, quietly collecting grime on their Victorian fronts. A half mile to the east was that brighter, newer, more sophisticated world we have seen at length, one that began rather abruptly with the Schenley Apartments and continued for a half mile more in a revel of architectural high style: Classicism of many varieties, Syrian Arabic, Prairie School, Arts and Crafts, and much else, with a stunning Gothic skyscraper as the mast around which all the rest gathered. As I grew a little older, I went to this different world more and more: to Schenley Park, the Carnegie Library of Pittsburgh and Carnegie Institute, or sometimes just to walk my grandfather home from his job at the Hotel Schenley late in the evening, usually carrying fresh-baked rolls not wanted for the dinners.

Pictured here around 1940 is your author's home at Fifth and Lothrop, with its three stories of dusty, dark green porches and its attendant basswoods and ailanthus. The Medical Center has now consumed everything within sight in this picture and, as I write, a tall, massive research laboratory is rising on this corner. The Oakland Civic Center is off to the right. (Pittsburgh History & Landmarks Foundation.)

It was a small-scale Victorian neighborhood, mostly, humble beneath the Pittsburgh soot. But eastward down Fifth Avenue were hints of the grander, newer, more famous Oakland. This was the 3600 block of Fifth Avenue in 1933. (Pittsburgh City Photographer Collection, Archives Service Center, University of Pittsburgh.)

Here is another view of this part of Fifth Avenue, just east of the Falk Clinic and the Children's Hospital. This shows the street in the early 1950s, not long before these buildings came down. (Carnegie Library of Pittsburgh.)

This is Bouquet Street, a little further east, again in the early 1950s. The Western State Psychiatric Hospital frowns upon houses that again were doomed. (The Historical Society of Western Pennsylvania.)

On this northern side of Fifth Avenue, and just across Bouquet Street, the glamorous showcase district was anticipated in the H. C. Frick School, a typically tasteful work in limestone from 1927 by Ingham & Boyd. (The Historical Society of Western Pennsylvania.)

Ingham & Boyd had to work around this embarrassing survivor from 1868: the old Bellefield School (or Fourteenth Ward, or Oakland School), which stood on the corner of Fifth and Thackeray until it burned out in 1957. (Pittsburgh City Photographer Collection, Archives Service Center, University of Pittsburgh.)

Across Thackeray Street was another Victorian survivor, the First United Presbyterian Church, a creditable if not glamorous Richardson Romanesque work of 1896, by Thomas Boyd. (Carnegie Library of Pittsburgh.)

Across Fifth Avenue from these modest beginnings was the motor entrance to the Schenley Apartments. Once there, you had definitely arrived in Pittsburgh's showplace. It all lay before you for the next half mile. (Pittsburgh History & Landmarks Foundation.)

Here are some other views of everyday Oakland. Two red-and-cream PCC trolleys on Forbes Street near Oakland Avenue are heading for Squirrel Hill. The year is 1945, and these streamlined trolleys are still in the process of replacing the familiar orange streetcars of the past. On the left, in the background, are the Iroquois Apartments. (Pittsburgh City Photographer Collection, Archives Service Center, University of Pittsburgh.)

The Iroquois Apartments were built in 1903 to designs by Frederick John Osterling. The apartment house was still a new genre in local architecture, though one becoming popular. The idea of persuading people to live under the same roof with strangers was a little challenging, and architects usually would either affect continental sophistication or suggest something English and manorial. Here, Osterling gave the Iroquois a look not out of place in upper Manhattan. (Pittsburgh History & Landmarks Foundation.)

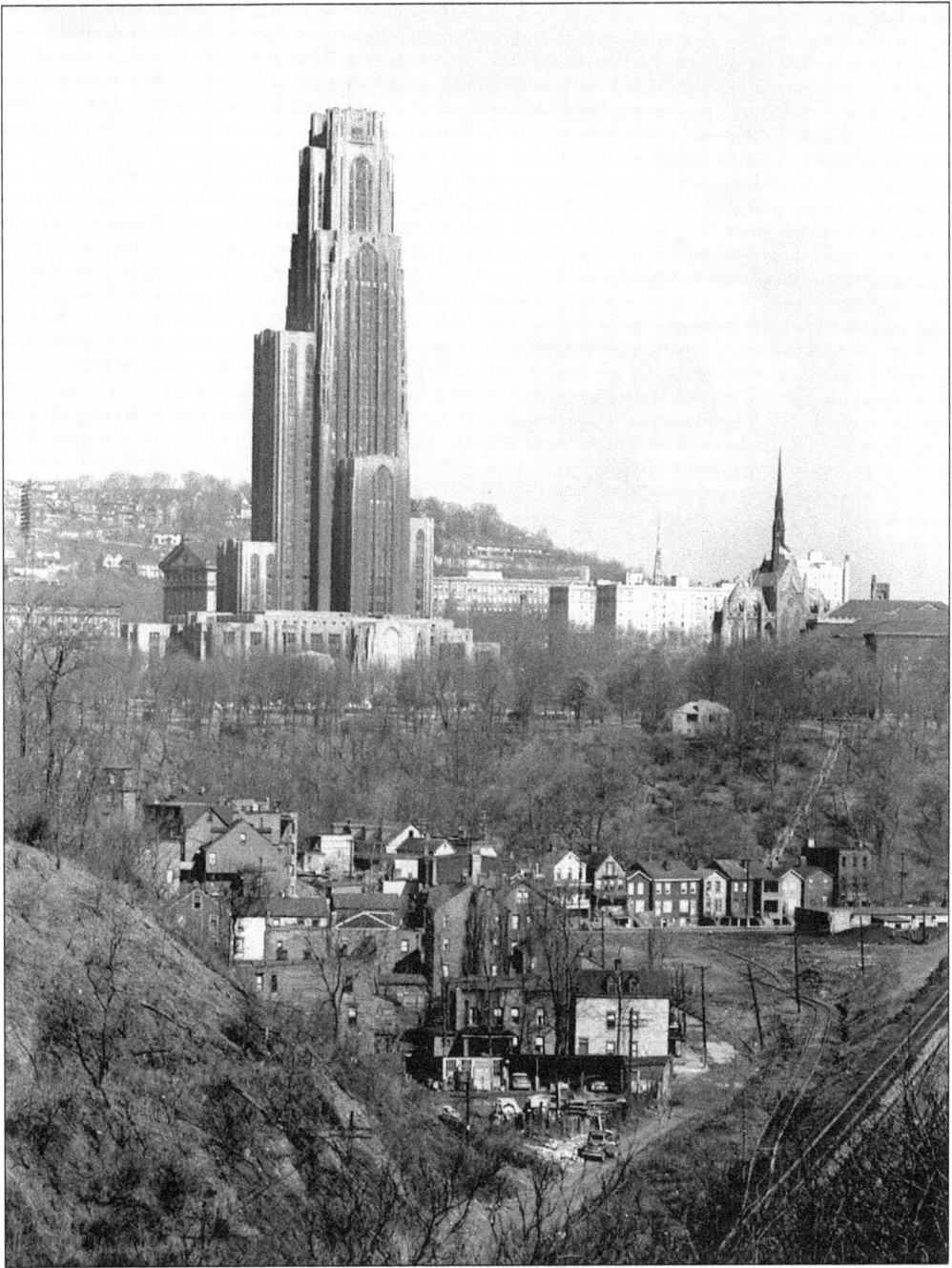

Junction Hollow offers extreme examples of the contrasts of Oakland. In this Harold Corsini view of 1953, we see the B&O Railroad branch that runs up the Hollow and the modest houses of Boundary Street near by. Above them, in another world, the Cathedral of Learning and the Heinz Chapel rise proudly. A straggling set of the public steps that are so numerous around Pittsburgh connects the two places. On the skyline to the left are houses of the Upper Hill. (Carnegie Library of Pittsburgh.)

And here is a similar contrast, with a little of the 1890s-period Oakland Square in the old Linden Grove part of South Oakland. At the far lower right are a few Boundary Street houses. The year is 1951, and the photographer is Clyde Hare, who had just begun his career of documenting the city. (Carnegie Library of Pittsburgh.)

In this view from the late 1920s from behind the Phipps Conservatory we see, from left to right, Forbes Field, the Schenley Hotel and Apartments, the Carnegie Library of Pittsburgh and Carnegie Institute building, and the Cathedral of Learning being framed up. (Carnegie Library of Pittsburgh.)

116

In this picture it is June 1914, looking north along Junction Hollow toward the Schenley Bridge, with a little of the Carnegie Library of Pittsburgh to the left, Machinery Hall of Carnegie Tech to the right, and Schenley Park just out of the picture to the right. (Pittsburgh City Photographer Collection, Archives Service Center, University of Pittsburgh.)

This is just a commonplace street scene, at Forbes Street near Halket, in September 1935. The Oakland Apartments stand to the left, with two 1870s-period mansard-roofed houses. The years have obviously been kind to none of them. The ailanthus tree grows weed like in front of one house, which has become the Elcarr Hotel for tourists, with rooms from 50¢ and up. (Pittsburgh City Photographer Collection, Archives Service Center, University of Pittsburgh.)

In South Oakland, row houses were common. Here is a view of 1932, looking up Juliet Street toward the Boulevard of the Allies. (Pittsburgh City Photographer Collection, Archives Service Center, University of Pittsburgh.)

And here are more genteel row houses on Coltart Square looking toward Bates Street in South Oakland. The year is 1910. (Pittsburgh City Photographer Collection, Archives Service Center, University of Pittsburgh.)

On the other hand, Oaklanders who worked in the riverside industrial plants long ascended the public steps to shabby houses that shared bare earth with privies and public water faucets. In this picture from 1952 we are looking down Maurice Street, which at this point is a long, straggling wooden stair, toward C. G. Hussey & Company's plant by the Monongahela. (Carnegie Library of Pittsburgh.)

Oakland's most conspicuous neighbors by the river were the Eliza Furnaces of the Jones & Laughlin Steel Company, "blown in" in 1861 and in production until 1979. They were among the first blast furnaces in the immediate Pittsburgh area, using coke—refined coal—rather than charcoal as fuel and supplied by rail and barge from mines up river. This is a view from 1935. (Pittsburgh City Photographer Collection, Archives Service Center, University of Pittsburgh.)

A few of the most notable Oakland institutions are pictured in the next photographs. St. Agnes Church, built in 1917 at the top of Soho Curve, acts almost as a formal introduction to the neighborhood as you approach from the west. It was the work of John Theodore Comes, one of the gifted architects for the Catholic Church who suddenly emerged at the beginning of the 20th century. (Catholic Diocese of Pittsburgh Archives and Records Center.)

120

On the hill above St. Agnes Church is Mount Mercy, successor to the Ursuline Young Ladies' Academy that we showed in the Soho Curve view from 1890. This is the convent, a work from 1886 by Joseph Stillburg, seen from Forbes Street and Craft Avenue. (Carnegie Library of Pittsburgh.)

This is Our Lady of Mercy Academy, now Carlow University, built next to the convent after the Ursulines left Oakland. (Carnegie Library of Pittsburgh.)

The First Congregational Church, on Dithridge Street near Forbes, was a sandstone-fronted gray brick building of 1904 by Thomas Hannah. It eventually became the St. Nicholas Greek Orthodox Cathedral. (Carnegie Library of Pittsburgh.)

The Tree of Life Synagogue was built on Craft Avenue early in 1907 to the designs of D. A. Crone. By 1951, when this picture was taken, the building was awaiting conversion for the Pittsburgh Playhouse. (The Historical Society of Western Pennsylvania.)

Among the schools of Oakland, after the University of Pittsburgh and Carnegie Institute of Technology, Schenley High School is the most prominent physically. The angle Bigelow Boulevard makes with Centre Avenue has given it the form of a scalene triangle with rounded corners. The architect was Edward Stotz. (Carnegie Library of Pittsburgh.)

Here, in 1925, a girls' gym team exercises next to Schenley High School's nearest neighbors along Bigelow Boulevard, at the edge of Schenley Farms. (Carnegie Library of Pittsburgh.)

In this view from 1917 we look toward Schenley High School. In the foreground are houses on North Craig Street, with North Dithridge Street beyond. To the left of the high school is the Western Pennsylvania Institution for the Blind, and to its right are Bellefield Dwellings, an early apartment house. The houses are very solidly middle class and in good condition, but gangly electric poles, conspicuous wires, and irregular tree planting show a marked contrast with the standards of Nicola's Schenley Farms, which lay just beyond the high school. (The Historical Society of Western Pennsylvania.)

The Western Pennsylvania Institution for the Blind, to become a neighbor of the Schenley Farms development, had been built on land donated by Mary Schenley. Designed by George Orth, who later had a society practice, it opened in 1894. (Pittsburgh History & Landmarks Foundation.)

Here is the corner of Centre Avenue, crossing the picture, with Bellefield Avenue heading south toward the Bellefield Presbyterian Church and the twin campanili of the Carnegie Library. Also conspicuous are the Hotel Schenley in the distance and the rear of the Western Pennsylvania Institution for the Blind a few hundred feet away. The year is about 1900. (Carnegie Library of Pittsburgh.)

A view from 1899 looks southeastward over Dithridge Street in the foreground and Craig Street beyond toward the future site of the Carnegie Institute of Technology, and toward Schenley Park and portions of Shadyside and Squirrel Hill. The long building in the middle distance has just become the Duquesne Garden sports arena. Across Craig Street, at the far right center, St. Paul's Cathedral will be built in a few years. (Pittsburgh History & Landmarks Foundation.)

The Alinda Preparatory School occupied one of the old Carrier houses at Fifth Avenue and Craig Street. We see some of its pupils in 1898. The car barn next door will become the Duquesne Garden. (The Historical Society of Western Pennsylvania.)

In 1900 the old Eichbaum House was approaching the last phase of its history, which had covered Oakland's existence, as the Pittsburg [sic] and Allegheny Free Kindergarten College. The house lasted into the 1920s, when it was about 80 years old and about as old as the neighborhood itself. Toward the end, according to a map, it was called The Fairview, and was presumably serving as an apartment house or residence. (The Historical Society of Western Pennsylvania.)

We end with a final contrast, one of architecture from the beginning of Pittsburgh's City Beautiful campaign with that of its climax—and, for that matter, of its effective end. The Hotel Schenley, brown brick and terra cotta, is finished off with the emphatic horizontal of a jutting, fretted cornice—still a Victorian building, rather phlegmatic in expression if elaborate in detail. It was a worldly building of its time. Behind it is the Cathedral of Learning, a strange, fanciful Gothic essay of complex, ascending masses faced in white limestone, a work of fictitious arches and abutments, a sort of habitable expressionist sculpture of courage and spirituality, victory and adventure: a dream. (Carnegie Library of Pittsburgh.)

128